RL

RUSHMORE
Wes Anderson
&
Owen Wilson

ff

faber and faber

First published in 1999
by Faber and Faber Limited
3 Queen Square London WC1N 3AU
Published in the United States by Faber and Faber, Inc.,
a division of Farrar, Straus and Giroux, Inc., New York

Photoset by Parker Typesetting Service, Leicester
Printed in England by Clays Ltd, St Ives plc

Special thanks to the great facilitator Jason Miller and to
Hunter Heller, Lindsey Berents-Weeramuni and
Lyndsay Freeman

A CIP record for this book
is available from the British Library

ISBN 0-571-20012-5

2 4 6 8 10 9 7 5 3

CONTENTS

FOREWORD

This story of Wes Anderson and Owen Wilson, 'the boys,' is a plucky tale of grit and high purpose. Wes and Owen are Texans and so their endless fascination with the ol' game of life (and the enormous sophistication of thought they bring to that game) is very often concealed behind tight-lipped rhetoric with a distinct sense of the absurd, the joke of it all, which they exhibit whenever there is danger in the air. Think Slim Pickens in *Dr Strangelove*. From past tours of Texas I had come to appreciate the heart of the state's culture long before I met the authors of *Bottle Rocket*. I was spoon-fed my most major Texas epiphany in one interview: a young man explained to me why he had fathered children when he was just past twenty, though he was fully aware that the decision meant shelving dreams and throwing out some fervent youthful ambitions to settle for doggedly making ends meet. His reason was: 'I want my children to have a real knowledge of their grandparents. So I had to have them early to give them the years.' Family, real and extended, is at the core of *Bottle Rocket*. Dignan (my vote for greatest first name in film) and Anthony are brothers in all respects save blood and, though separable, their tie is indestructible.

So it is with the co-authors of *Bottle Rocket*, Wes Anderson (also the director) and Owen Wilson (also the star). The other star of the film is Luke Wilson, Owen's brother; two other key cast members are Andrew Wilson, also a brother, and Bob Musgrave, a lifelong friend. All of them lived together in a glop in the same Houston apartment when I first met them. Now that Wes has distinguished himself as one of the leading young directors in film, and Owen and Luke have become respected, sought-after and very highly paid actors, they all have naturally gone upscale. These days they live together in a glop in Hollywood.

To get through the stuff of publicity releases as quickly as possible: *Bottle Rocket* was born as a ten-minute video shown at Sundance (it finished third at some festival for shorts). They had been mentored for a year by producer Barbara Boyle and writer

Kit Carson. Barbara brought the short and the resulting full-length screenplay to Polly Platt, an associate of mine, who championed it to me and urged me to go down to Texas to meet with 'the boys,' after which we brought Wes and Owen to Hollywood, where they spent a solid year rewriting and another year making the picture which was released to critical acclaim.

When I first saw the ten-minute video I was dazzled – the language and rhythms of the piece made it clear Wes and Owen were genuine voices. The possession of a real voice is always a marvel, an almost religious thing. When you have one, it not only means you see things from a slightly different perspective than the billions of other ants on the hill, but that you also necessarily possess such equally rare qualities as integrity and humility. It's part of the package of being a real voice, 'cause when your voice is real, you can't screw around. The voice must be served; all other exit doors marked 'expediency' or 'solid career move' are sealed over and the only way out of your inner torment is genuine self-expression.

So, I'm in Houston meeting 'the boys' who had done the short and I suggest that the next morning we should read the script aloud. They were so raw and new at writing and directing that it had never occurred to them to read the script aloud even though practically the entire cast lived in the same glop of humanity and was never unavailable. Wes and Owen figured you write it, you sell it and then make it or die. Reading it aloud was frou-frou.

When we conducted the reading we discovered, for reasons I'll never fully understand, that an ordinary number of script pages had produced the longest entertainment known to man, beating Wagner's *Ring* cycle before we reached the halfway point of the reading. By the time we approached the last scene all the water pitchers had been emptied yet voices still rasped from overuse, and there were people in the room showing the physical signs of starvation. Finally it was over. I nodded at everyone; the truth was so obvious no words were needed. I thought, from my Hollywood perch, that it had been an enormously revealing exercise, clearly showing the staging ground for the next draft.

The appropriate dialogue was for Wes and Owen to thank me for the revelation of my suggested reading and for them to contact me in three or four years after they'd blasted through the mountain of words and laid out some sort of narrative road. We said our goodbyes and I walked across the street when Wes loudly blurted for me to wait. He crossed to me and stood very close. In the years I've known him since, I don't think he ever again stood quite so close. 'Are you going to make the movie?' he asked. I started to answer that it was impossible to tell at this point. But he interrupted my preamble. 'Are you going to make the movie?' he asked again. I started to answer anew and then realized this very basic question was such a matter of survival to him that he simply couldn't endure any long-winded answer. So I said, 'I don't know, man.' He nodded and walked away.

Not long thereafter we brought Wes and Owen from Houston to Hollywood. They were given offices on the Sony Studios lot. They were in their early twenties and had a script deal. They now slumbered in the very belly of the beast they had coveted since they first met in a play-writing workshop at the University of Texas. They were film guys now to the IRS as well as to themselves and their parents. They had imagined this life from afar for so long that now with actual physical contact with the movie industry they had lusted after and its powerful seductions, there was the distinct danger of the boys going wrong. Not to worry. Somehow these guys arrived in town with a concrete bunker protecting their cores.

Their first brushes with agents and execs left them without a dent. Wes's persona was a major help. No matter what they thought of him in the jock-infested world of his youth, here in Hollywood he was an intimidating presence. First off, he looked like a genius. There was some Einstein thing with his hair, plus he was rickets-thin and shabbily dressed. When he looked at agents and did that long think thing before saying any words at all, you could see the sweat staining the Egyptian cotton of the agents' shirts. Yes, it was the sharpies who began to break and stammer and attempt to change their styles under the unblinking gaze of the two newcomers.

I worked with Wes and Owen for the better and worser part of a year and they were like no writing team I'd ever encountered. First of all, you could never catch them communicating with each other in front of you. Nor could you pressure them into actually expressing an individual reaction on the spot to something you said. Yet they weren't rude. It was some trick or talent and it was always there, always. I would pitch some idea or notion about a scene and there it would end. One of them might jot a note but that was it. And it's not as if I didn't prod them with a 'So what do you think?' And it wasn't silence that came back from such direct assaults, at least not technically, because words were muttered by them. But never words that fit together in anything resembling declarative thought. Our times were pleasant enough; Owen is a great laugher. I never in my life met anyone who laughed more often and still seemed genuinely surprised every time he did.

When the script was finished and we were all set to go, we ran into a solid wall of resistance. Even with a lot of experience, I did not see the problem coming. It took every flex of every muscle our small but not insignificant film company, Gracie Film, had to get the powers that be to cough up the five million dollars needed to produce this highly personal film. But cough they finally did, and after well over a year, 'the boys' were back in Texas; this time to direct and star in a major studio picture.

Early in the course of the actual film-making that which could not be foreseen became wildly apparent. Wes and Owen knew their stuff. Owen proved as an actor, as well as a writer, to be incapable of a dishonest moment. Wes, who unquestionably fretted mightily through every moment of the day, still maintained the outward appearance of cool control. He was sure-handed and knowing in all aspects of directing. He was – as they call everyone who has killed themselves preparing in every conceivable way for what may be their one and only shot at the only job they imagine – a natural.

Nonetheless, the finish of principal photography led only to the toughest mettle tests to date. The film's test previews were torture. Richard Sakai, one of the producers and the head of our little company, held the film's coterie together. He does not rattle and after such screenings we'd cluster around him, frequently unable to locate Wes. This personal, spirited, original piece of work was walking exactly the same market testing plank as big Hollywood genre pics. Oh, God, what had we done to them? They had been safe in Texas. Owen worked at Blockbuster in Houston so 'the boys' had free movies every night, they were within driving distance of their Mom and Dad's, they had their buddies, the constant energetic dialogues planning their futures. Now there was only the din of dashed hopes.

Bottle Rocket was written off. I think the boys felt it and I knew it cold. Some connected with the movie drifted away to nurse their pain; others, most notably Richard, never wavered.

Wes and Owen kept working on the film, though. Wes's fears enlarged until the only decent thing to do was lie to him. '*ET* had terrible previews,' we declared. 'Everyone thought the creature was a weak crybaby always wanting to go home. Then they got a good music score and some nice lettering for the main titles and that did the trick.'

But finally, though seriously rattled, Wes and Owen were sustained by the work. They never lost their hold on the truth. They had got to do the jobs they loved. Finally, that is the edge. Wes managed to get a great and appropriate score for less money than anyone would have thought possible. And in this experience, as in virtually all other areas of post-production, someone like music editor Kim Naves would see the film and go nuts over it and the reaction would pick everyone up. The studio gave us the funds for another couple of days of shooting. Owen and Wes went off to write a new opening, and despite the pressure, they were once more buoyant from being able to write some scenes and then film them. It was getting Capraesque. Even I was feeling the glow. Lord love our noble little group and the film we served.

In the middle of all this heart, drive and renewal, the cruelest of events stopped us in our tracks. *Bottle Rocket,* the child of the Sundance Shorts Program, was disowned and disinherited by the Sundance Film Festival. The festival refused to admit the film in its competition. This rejection hit the boys harder than anything else. The very people for whom they felt greatest fealty cast them out. The rejection rocked their cage. I felt enraged and helpless. But I think the truly awful things in life, when they occur, bring with them the call to dignity. Owen and Wes conducted themselves with extraordinary elan. They took the full hit of the turn-down, conceded the pain and confusion it caused them and recommitted themselves to the work.

Some months later the movie opened without benefit of a festival foothold. Kenneth Turan's *Los Angeles Times* review said in part, '*Bottle Rocket* has just what its characters lack; an exact sense of itself. A confident, eccentric debut about a trio of shambling and guileless friends who become the Candides of crime, *Rocket* feels particularly refreshing because it never compromises on its delicate deadpan sensibility. Unlike most lost generation tales, this one never loses its way. Inexplicably, almost criminally turned down by the Sundance Film Festival, *Bottle Rocket* is especially exciting because it was put together by a core group of under-thirties, all of whom are new to features . . . Here's hoping there are others out there this fresh and this bright.'

The film received any number of selections to Ten Best lists, standing alongside such films of that year as *The English Patient*, *Jerry Maguire* and *Fargo*.

Bottle Rocket was not a commercial success but it was celebrated and embraced by a core of passionate fans, and the critical benedictions launched three careers. Owen and Wes went to work writing *Rushmore*, which, at the time of writing, has been hailed in three film festivals: Telluride, Toronto and New York. Luke and Owen Wilson are sought-after actors and Wes Anderson is now an established director.

The Turan review (and others like it) without exaggeration saved Wes and Owen's lives, for life can be very tough on those who find existence only makes sense if someone lets them make movies. The lack of a logical alternative creates more peril than opportunity. The rites of passage Wes and Owen moved through during the time we worked on *Bottle Rocket* were brutal.

They have pulled off the hardest trick of all in contemporary American film: they have won the freedom to use movies as a form of self-expression. Frequently, writers and directors, in order to maintain employability, hold to a career course of 'One for us and one for them,' meaning alternately suffocating one's own tastes to do the system's bidding in the preposterous belief that the system, in return, will allow the search for artistic fulfillment on alternate jobs. Wes and Owen need not walk that screwy path. They have no choice but to keep things simple. They will do their act. If they weren't writing their scripts nothing at all like those scripts would exist. And I believe such will always be the case for 'the boys.' Wow.

James L. Brooks, 1998

INTRODUCTION

I wanted to show our movie to Pauline Kael. I already had her phone number because I'd found it when I was looking through somebody's Rolodex a couple of years ago, so I called her.

'Hello. My name is Wes Anderson. I'm calling for Pauline Kael, please.' I had immediately recognized her voice (from a tape I have of her on the Dick Cavett show) when she answered the telephone, but I wanted to give her a chance to introduce herself. What follows is my recollection of our conversation.*

'Who *are* you?' she said suspiciously and steely. I paused.

'I'm a film-maker, and I've just finished a movie called *Rushmore*, and I was hoping maybe I could –'

'How long is it?'

'Ninety minutes.'

'Ninety?'

'Or slightly less. Ninety-ish,' I said.

'That's a long *Rushmore*.'

I hesitated. I thought she was making a joke, but I didn't get it. I said, 'Well, it's got a pretty quick pace.'

'What'd you do on it?'

'I directed it.'

'Who wrote it?'

'Me and my friend Owen Wilson.'

'Who's in it?'

'Bill Murray.' This was my trump card. I knew from her reviews that Bill Murray is one of her favorite comedians.

'Which Bill Murray?'

There was a silence. '*The* Bill Murray. You know Bill Murray. You *love* Bill Murray.'

'What was he in?'

My mind drew a blank. 'What was he in?' I repeated the

* I sent this piece to Kael for her remarks. She read it and called me and suggested four changes. I have footnoted each of them. The first was that I should add this sentence: 'What follows is my recollection of our conversation.' (She says that I have occasionally paraphrased her.)

question. I could only think of one title. '*Meatballs*,' I said.

It didn't ring a bell. 'You'll know him when you see him.'

She laughed uncomfortably and said, 'OK.' She asked if *Rushmore* was my first film, and I told her no, that I'd directed a movie called *Bottle Rocket*.

There was another silence.

'Well, let's hope this one's not too thrown together.'

I thought about this. 'How do you mean "thrown together"?' I said.

She didn't answer. I waited. She laughed quietly, and then she seemed to warm up all of the sudden: 'OK, send me the tape,' she said.*

'Actually, to tell you the truth, I'd prefer to screen it for you. Is there a movie theater near you?'

She paused. 'There's the Triplex.'

'Let me show it to you at the Triplex.'

She sounded skeptical. 'How are we going to do that?'

'I'll get the studio to set it up.'

'That could be expensive,' she said.

'Well. Let's stick it to them,' I said.

She liked the sound of this. 'OK, let's stick it to them,' she said. She told me she didn't drive, and that someone would have to pick her up and take her to the theater.

I said, 'I'll do it myself. How do I get to your house?'

'I don't know,' she said.

'OK. I'll figure it out.'

The arrangements were made, and a few weeks later I drove from Cambridge to Kael's house in Great Barrington, Massachusetts. I brought some cookies with me which I thought I would offer her during the first reel.

Her house is clapboard† and very large, and I saw a deer duck into the trees at the corner of the yard as I came up the driveway. I knocked on the screen door and she looked out at me. She was sitting in a wooden chair. 'My God, you're just a kid,' she said.

---

* Kael later clarified her reaction to *Bottle Rocket* for me. She said, 'It *was* thrown together, but it had some nice parts.' I repeated this back to her:

'It was thrown together, but it had a few good parts.'

'No,' she said. 'It had *some* nice parts. That's better than a few.'

† Kael tells me that the house is actually 'stone and shingle.'

She told me to open the door. I tried it. I told her it was locked. She told me the lock had been broken for twenty years,* and that I should just fiddle with it. She said she knew it was twenty years because she'd just finished paying off her mortgage.

I fiddled with the lock for a minute and got the door open. We shook hands and I said, 'It's very nice to meet you. How are you?'

'Old,' she said.

She was a few inches under five feet tall, and she stood shakily with a metal cane that had four legs at the base. We both had on New Balance sneakers.

She has Parkinson's, which makes her shake a little bit and leaves her unsteady. She told me she had been in the hospital with meningitis during the week after we spoke on the telephone, which explained her forgetting who Bill Murray is. She told me I would have to hold her hand and help her get around, and I told her that would be just fine. We made our way out to the car.

On the way to the theater she told me she'd invited her friend Dorothy to join us. 'I would've gotten a group together, but I didn't want to have too many people, in case the movie isn't any good.'

I nodded and pulled into the driveway next to the theater. There was a little small-town police station there, and I stopped in front of it.

'You can't park here, Wes.'

'Oh, I think we'll be OK.'

She shook her head. She said this was proof that I was a movie director. No one else would think they could double-park in front of a police station.

I got out of the car and went to open Kael's door. A police officer came out of the station and told me to move my car, and I told him I was just going to walk Ms Kael into the movie theater first. He watched me coldly. Kael kept shaking her head.

We went into the lobby and she introduced me to Dorothy. 'This is Wes Anderson. He's responsible for whatever it is we're about to see.' Kael told me she thought I should change my name. 'Wes Anderson is a terrible name for a movie director.'

Dorothy agreed.

* Kael says, 'The lock has been *stiff* for twenty years, not broken.'

I ran out to move the car, and then I went up to the projection booth to tell the projectionist we were ready. I came back down and found Kael and Dorothy sitting near the back of the theater. Kael explained, 'I like to see the whole screen.' I offered them some cookies, and Kael immediately started eating one. 'These don't have butter in them, do they?'

'My guess is they probably do,' I said.

'I'm not supposed to eat butter,' she said, but she kept eating the cookies. Then we started the movie. Kael and Dorothy watched for an hour in total silence. Then Dorothy, who is a real estate agent, got paged and walked out, and that was the last I saw of her. Finally the movie ended, and I took Kael's hand and walked with her out of the theater.

'I don't know what you've got here, Wes.'

I nodded.

'Did the people who gave you the money read the script?'

I frowned. 'Yeah. That's kind of their policy.'

We started slowly down the steps. 'Just asking,' she said. It was a short walk to the car. 'At this point I would usually tell you not to worry if you have to carry me, since I only weigh eighty-five pounds. But you look like you don't weigh much more than that yourself.'

I didn't say anything. I helped her into the car, put her aluminum cane in back, and closed the door.

I was a little disappointed by Kael's reaction to the movie. She is probably the most influential movie critic of all time, and she is definitely my favorite. I started reading her *New Yorker* reviews in my school library when I was in tenth grade, and her books were always my main guide for finding the right movies to watch and learning about film-makers. I'd gone to great lengths to arrive at this moment. I got in the car, and she closed the case on the subject: 'I genuinely don't know what to make of this movie,' she said, and I felt she meant it.

I drove us back to her house. We went inside, and Kael invited me to sit with her in her study and talk.

On the way upstairs she clutched the bannister and told me she wished there were bannisters everywhere – on sidewalks, in restaurants, etc. 'They're so great,' she said.

The house is full of books, and the rooms are large, with lots of windows. She took me to a closet in a room so crammed with tall stacks of boxes that you had to turn sideways to squeeze around them. The closet had extra copies of all her books. She told me I could have any of them I wanted. They were first editions, and I wanted to take a dozen of them, but eventually I just chose two.

I asked her to sign one of them for me, and she said this would take a few minutes. Her Parkinson's makes it difficult for her to write. That's why she quit *The New Yorker*. I asked her if she'd ever dictated a review, and she said, 'I think I wrote more with my hand than with my brain.' She said she would never write again.

'Glad to hear it,' I said, thinking of the review of *Rushmore* that she wasn't going to write. She looked up at me. She smiled faintly.

Then we sat for a while talking about movies, and she finished signing my book, and I told her I had to get back on the road. I was headed for New York, and it was already getting dark out.

She walked me to the door, and we chatted a little longer. She told me to keep in touch, and we said goodbye. I didn't look at her inscription in my book until I'd checked into my hotel room in Manhattan. It said:

> For Wes Anderson,
> With affection and a few queries.
> Pauline Kael

Owen Wilson and I would like to dedicate this volume to Pauline Kael, with great affection and a few queries of our own.

Wes Anderson, 1998

Rushmore

INT. CLASSROOM – DAY

A private day school. Twenty tenth-grade boys are sitting in desks in geometry class. They are dressed in school uniform, light blue shirts and khakis. The boys look dazed and sleepy.

The teacher, Mr Adams, is at the front of the room, finishing a complicated equation on the chalkboard.

> MR ADAMS
>
> Except when the value of the x co-ordinate is less than or equal to the value of the – Yes, Isaac?

A boy named Isaac has raised his hand.

> ISAAC
>
> What about that problem?

Isaac points to a startling and intricate arrangement of numbers and symbols filling up a forgotten corner of the chalkboard. The heading above it says 'Extra Credit'.

> MR ADAMS
>
> Oh, I really just put that up there as a joke. That's probably the hardest geometry equation in the world.

> ISAAC
>
> How much extra credit is it worth?

> MR ADAMS
>
> Well. I've never seen anyone get it right before, including my mentor Dr Leaky at MIT. So I guess if anyone here can do it,
>
> *(pause)*
>
> I'll make sure none of you ever have to open another math book again for the rest of your lives.

There is some quiet murmuring. The name Fischer is repeated over and over. The boys begin to look to a student in the back row.

3

*Unlike his classmates, he wears the Rushmore school blazer with
insignia on the breast pocket and a Rushmore rep tie knotted tightly.
His hair is smartly parted and swept back. He is extremely skinny and
pale. He is Max Fischer.*

Max has a cup of coffee on his desk and he is reading the Wall Street
Journal.

MR ADAMS

Max? You want to try it?

Max looks up.

MAX

I'm sorry. Did someone say my name?

*Everyone laughs. Max smiles slightly. He buttons his blazer and
straightens his tie. His picks up his cup of coffee and takes a sip. He goes
to the chalkboard and sets to work.*

*The boys watch with nervous anticipation. Mr Adams compares Max's
progress with the notes in his book. Max's equation quickly fills up most
of the board. He finishes it with a flourish, throws his piece of chalk in
the trash, and turns to face the class.*

Everyone looks to Mr Adams. Mr Adams raises an eyebrow. He nods.

*The classroom erupts into wild, ecstatic applause. Everyone surrounds
Max, cheering, as he walks calmly back to his desk. They hoist him into
the air.*

CUT TO:

*Max with his eyes closed, smiling serenely, listening to the applause. He
mutters:*

MAX

Gentlemen, gentlemen, please.

*A little hand grabs Max's arm and shakes him. Max opens his eyes.
The person shaking him is his chapel partner, Dirk Calloway, a fourth
grader with nearly white hair. Max looks around.*

*They are in chapel, surrounded by rows of boys in school uniforms. Dirk
puts his finger to his lips.*

4

Shh.

Max rubs his eyes and sits up in the pew. The applause dies down and Max looks to the pulpit as the guest chapel speaker, Herman Blume, steps up to the microphone.

Mr Blume is a tough-looking guy about fifty years old in a black suit. He begins his chapel speech.

MR BLUME

You guys have it real easy. I never had it like this where I grew up. But I send my kids here. Because the fact is, whether you deserve it or not: you go to one of the best schools in this country.

Max's eyes light up.

MR BLUME

Rushmore. You lucked out.

Max leans forward to the railing and begins to listen intently.

Now for some of you it doesn't matter. You were born rich and you're going to stay rich. But here's my advice to the rest of you: take dead aim on the rich boys. Get them in the crosshairs. And *take them down*.

Some of the students and faculty begin to look at each other with puzzled expressions. Max is nodding and taking notes on the flypage of a hymnal.

INSERT HYMNAL:

> Rushmore – best school in country.
> rich kids – bad?

MR BLUME

Just remember: they can buy anything. But they can't buy backbone. Don't let them forget it. Thank you.

Mr Blume leaves the podium. Max leaps to his feet and leads the applause. The organ starts and everyone stands up.

EXT. QUADRANGLE – DAY

Mr Blume and the headmaster, Dr Guggenheim, come out of the chapel among the throng of students.

Dr Guggenheim wears a wool coat and smokes a pipe. He is very dashing with silver hair and a warmly patronizing manner. He walks with his hands clasped behind his back.

Two Jack Russell terriers follow quickly at his heels.

DR GUGGENHEIM

Are you free for graduation, Herman? Maybe you could give us an encore.
    (whistles to the dogs)
Nicholas! Copernicus!

MR BLUME
(lighting a cigarette)
I don't give a shit. I paid for the whole damn natatorium. The least these little pricks can do is hear me out.

MAX

Mr Blume.

Max has appeared beside them. Dirk tags along behind him.

My name's Max Fischer. I just wanted to tell you, I strongly agree with your views concerning Rushmore.

MR BLUME

You don't say. Tell me something. How long have you gone
here?

MAX

Ten years.

MR BLUME

Then you've been in a dreamworld for ten years.

MAX

I know it, sir.

*Max smiles broadly. They each notice that their haircuts are identical,
neatly parted on the side.*

Your speech was excellent. Except I disagree with your ideas
about rich kids. Because, after all, we don't choose who our
fathers are. But that's really my only criticism.

MR BLUME
(*hesitates*)

Thank you.

Mr Blume looks at Dirk staring up at him. Dirk says softly:

DIRK

Hello.

MAX

This is my chapel partner, Dirk Calloway.

MR BLUME
(*shakes Dirk's hand*)

Nice to meet you, Dirk.

MAX

Thank you for coming today, sir.

*Max shakes Mr Blume's hand. Mr Blume smiles. But Max doesn't go.
He just stands there. Searching for the words.*

I really. I think it's. You're right about Rushmore. Look
around. It truly is a great school.

Mr Blume nods. A little uneasy.

7

Anyway. Nice to have met you.

Max goes. Mr Blume and Dr Guggenheim watch him walk away with Dirk.

                              MR BLUME
What's his name again?

                          DR GUGGENHEIM
Max Fischer.

                              MR BLUME
He's a sharp little guy.

Dr Guggenheim looks across the lawn at Max and his chapel partner. He says wistfully:

                          MR GUGGENHEIM
He's one of the worst students we've got.

INSERT COVER OF THE RUSHMORE YEARBOOK:

It is called the Rushmore Yankee. *The masthead says Max is editor-in-chief. There is a photograph of him laughing, surrounded by his staff.*

We cut to a series of pictures of:

The French Club, Debate Team, cross-country, lacrosse, golf, drama, Astronomy Society, Glee Club, student council, Model United Nations, Stamp & Coin Club, Gun Club, Bombardment Society, calligraphy, fencing, kung fu, bee-keeping, and J. V. water polo.

YANKEE RACERS
FOUNDER

8

Max is president or captain of virtually every one of these.

*Other photographs show Max pole-vaulting, dancing at the Christmas
Ball, and giving a thumbs-up from the cockpit of a Piper Cub.*

TITLE:

September.

INT. DR GUGGENHEIM'S OFFICE – DAY

*A paneled room with wooden floors, an old electric fan on the
windowsill, and paintings of ducks and geese on the walls. Dr
Guggenheim is seated at his little oak desk. Max sits across from him in
an antique leather armchair.*

DR GUGGENHEIM
We're putting you on what we call sudden death academic
probation.

MAX
(*nodding*)
And what does that entail?

DR GUGGENHEIM
It entails that if you fail another class you're going to be asked
to leave Rushmore.

MAX
I see.
(*raises an eyebrow*)
In other words, I'll be expelled.

DR GUGGENHEIM
Right.

Silence.

MAX
Dr Guggenheim. I don't want to tell you how to do your job.
But the fact is no matter how hard I try I still might flunk
another class. And if that means I have to stay on for a
postgraduate year, then so be it. But if –

9

DR GUGGENHEIM
We don't offer a postgraduate year.

MAX
Well. We don't offer it *yet.*
(*pause*)
And what about the fact that I'm probably dyslexic?

DR GUGGENHEIM
You're not dyslexic.

MAX
Well, I'm a terrible speller.

DR GUGGENHEIM
Just bring up the grades.

Max sighs. He looks out the window and says quietly:

MAX
You remember how I got into this school?

DR GUGGENHEIM
Yes, I do. You wrote a play.

MAX
That's right. A little one act. About Watergate. And my mother read it and felt I should go to Rushmore. And you read it and you gave me a scholarship, didn't you?

Dr Guggenheim nods.

Do you regret it?

DR GUGGENHEIM
No, I don't regret it. But I still might have to expel you.

Max nods. He smiles sadly and whispers:

MAX
Couldn't we just let me float by? For old times' sake?

DR GUGGENHEIM
(*grimly*)
Can't do it, Max.

EXT. QUADRANGLE – DAY

Max and Dirk come out the door into the cold. They head across the grass.

MAX

They want to kick me out, Dirk.

DIRK
(*concerned*)

Oh, no. Not again. What are you going to do?

MAX

The only thing I *can* do. Try to pull some strings with the administration, I guess.

DIRK

Maybe you ought to get a tutor.

MAX

I don't have time for a goddamn tutor. You know my schedule.

INSERT SIGN WRITTEN IN CALLIGRAPHY:

BACKGAMMON CLUB
Founder: Max Fischer.

INT. LIBRARY – DAY

A long table in the Rushmore library. Max is reading a library copy of a book about Jacques Cousteau. He is also playing backgammon with a freshman named Alex.

ALEX

Did you hear they're teaching Japanese next year?

MAX

That's the rumor.

ALEX

And they're canceling Latin.

MAX

What? I tried to get Latin canceled for five years. It's a dead language, I'd always say.

ALEX

Well, I guess they finally heard you.

Max shakes his head as this sinks in.

MAX

At least I saved Dirk from the horror.

Max turns the page of his book. There is a photograph of Jacques Cousteau laughing uproariously. A little note is written in pencil in the margin next to it with an arrow pointing to the picture. Max frowns. He turns the book sideways to read it.

INSERT FRAGMENT OF NOTE IN BOOK:

When one person, for whatever reason,
has a chance to lead an exceptional life,
he has no right to keep it to himself.
– Jacques Cousteau

Max's frown disappears. A change comes over his face. His eyes glaze over dreamily. He whispers to Alex:

MAX

Read this.

Alex reads the quote. He looks puzzled.

ALEX

What's that supposed to mean?

MAX
(*mysteriously*)

I don't know. Maybe nothing. Excuse me, please.

Max gets up and goes to the checkout counter. He shows the book to the Librarian.

I'd like to see a list of all the people who've checked-out this book in the past year.

LIBRARIAN

Why?

Max points to the quote. The librarian reads it. She nods. She goes through the cards in a little wooden box.

INSERT SCRAP OF PAPER:

Miss Cross, 1st grade, room 121

INT. HALLWAY — DAY

Max walks down a hallway in the lower school. He is carrying the little scrap of paper, checking room numbers as he walks.

He looks in some of the rooms. He sees kids sitting at tables with scissors and paste. Kids watching a movie on science. Kids curled-up on mats during naptime.

And then he sees room 121. He goes to the door and looks through the window.

A class of first graders are sitting Indian-style in a little circle on the floor. The teacher is in a tiny little kid's chair, reading aloud from Kidnapped. *She is twenty-eight. She wears a cardigan sweater and her hair is pulled back like a ballet dancer. She is Miss Cross.*

Max's eyes are glued to the glass. He cracks open the door an inch to listen to her voice.

> MISS CROSS
> I have seen wicked men and fools, a great many of both; and I believe they both get paid in the end.
> (*darkly*)
> But the fools first.

She looks up mysteriously. She turns the page and continues:

Chapter fifteen. 'The Lad with the Silver Button'.

INT. BLUME INTERNATIONAL CONCRETE — DAY

Mr Blume has a gigantic office with paintings of battle scenes and Viking ships, a coat of armor, and a statue of a discus thrower. The concrete plant is outside the window.

A portrait of the Blume family hangs on the wall behind Mr Blume's desk. His wife and twin sons are all fair-skinned redheads. Mr Blume is dark and sullen. He is smoking a cigarette in the painting.

Mr Blume sits at his desk with a silver military issue .45 automatic disassembled in front of him. He is cleaning it and drinking a Bloody Mary. His Secretary buzzes him on the speakerphone. Mr Blume pushes a button on it.

MR BLUME

Yeah?

SECRETARY

Mrs Blume wants you to pick up the twins from school at 3:15.

MR BLUME

Tell them to take a cab, and I'll reimburse them this evening.

INT. CAR – DAY

Max is sitting in a parked Jaguar with Dirk's mother, Mrs Calloway. She is beautiful. She is dressed in tennis clothes and wears a terrycloth visor.

Max is wearing a fluorescent orange crossing guard's belt with a badge at the shoulder that says Patrol Chief. He hands Mrs Calloway his phone number.

MRS CALLOWAY

Thank you, Max. I was just telling Mr Calloway the other day how fortunate we are to have someone like you looking out for Dirk.

MAX

My pleasure. I'm just trying to impart some of the experiences I've accrued to help Dirk. There he is now. Nice talking with you, Mrs Calloway.

They shake hands. Max gets out of the car and puts his hand on Dirk's shoulder.

How'd the math test go?

DIRK

What math test?

14

MAX

I thought you had a math test.

DIRK

No. Did you turn in your paper on the Berlin Airlift?

MAX

Yeah. I got an extension.

Dirk gets in the car and drives off. A seventh grader named Bobby goes over to Max.

BOBBY

How'd it go?

MAX

I shook hands with her.

BOBBY

Big deal.

MAX

And I gave her my phone number.

BOBBY

Buchan said he'd have already banged her by now.

MAX

He said that?

Max looks across the yard at Magnus Buchan, the burly foreign-exchange student from Scotland. He is seventeen. He has a straw in his mouth, and he shoots a small blowdart at a little kid's neck.

Half of Buchan's ear was blown off in a hunting accident.

That's a really crude thing to say. That's Dirk's mother.

BOBBY

But I thought that's why you picked Dirk as your chapel partner.

MAX

(*looks at Bobby, pause*)

What are you, a lawyer? All I'm saying is that gorilla is a guest

15

at our school for the year, so respect our women the same way we would in his jerkwater country.

Mr Blume pulls up in a brand new black Bentley.

Mr Blume!

Max goes over to Mr Blume's car.

It's Max Fischer.

MR BLUME
(*weary*)

Hi, Max.

They shake hands through the open car window.

MAX

How's the concrete business?

MR BLUME

Oh, I don't know. By the time you hit forty-five you've been fucked over so many times you don't really care anymore.

MAX
(*pause*)

I'm sorry to hear that.

Mr Blume sighs deeply. He stares out the windshield.

MRS BLUME

What's the secret, Max?

MAX

The secret?

MR BLUME

Yeah. You look like you've got it all figured out.

MAX

I don't know. I think you just got to find something you love to do, then do it for the rest of your life.
(*shrugs*)
For me, it's going to Rushmore.

Max looks very serious. Mr Blume smiles and nods.

Hey, Ronny. Hey, Donny.

Mr Blume's red-headed twins Ronny and Donny come over to the car.
They're Max's age but much more thick and solid.

> RONNY

Shotgun.

Donny gets in the front seat anyway. Ronny hollers:

I said shotgun, Donny!

> MR BLUME

Get in the back, Ronny.

Donny punches three different buttons on the dash that crank up the AC
full blast. Mr Blume's hair dances in the cold burst of air. He shuts off
the AC.

> MAX

See you tomorrow, Mr Blume.
> *(looks off)*

Mrs Reynolds!

Max goes to shake hands with somebody else's parents. Mr Blume looks
after Max fondly.

> MR BLUME

Did you invite that kid to the party?

> DONNY
> *(shocked)*

Max Fischer?

> RONNY

Come on, Dad. There's going to be girls there.

> DONNY

Pull your head out of your ass.

Mr Blume turns on Donny quickly like he is going to attack him.
Donny cowers grinning in the backseat with his fists up. Ronny pipes in:

> RONNY

Remember what Mom said. Hugs not hits.

17

INT. AUDITORIUM – DAY

The school auditorium. The stage is bare except for two folding chairs. A tall senior plays Frank. He is wearing a stocking cap and sunglasses. A fat kid plays Willie.

> FRANK

Wait a second. What time did the old lady place the 911 call?

> WILLIE

Ten-fifteen.

> FRANK
> (*snaps his fingers*)

That's it.

Frank jumps out of his seat.

Meet me on the corner in ten minutes.

> WILLIE

Where're you going?

> FRANK

I'll tell you in the squad car.

He heads toward the wings, then stops.

Oh, and, Willie. You were wrong about Enrique Sanchez. He died in his sleep.

He exits.

> MAX

Excellent!

Willie looks into the darkness beyond the stage. Max emerges and quickly climbs the steps onto the stage. He is followed by Dirk who is holding a script.

Excellent. Irving?

The stage manager is a wavy-haired sophomore named Irving. He comes out from backstage. Max pulls some money out of his pocket and hands it to him.

Get some root beers for anybody who wants one. I don't want one. OK. Next scene.

(*looks at Dirk's script*)

Frank. You enter stage right with the bag of cocaine.

INT. BARBER'S SHOP — DAY

A small, clean barber's shop. Mr Fischer is a white-haired man of sixty-five in a white barber's shirt. He has just finished giving a buzzcut to a twelve year-old boy named Gordon.

GORDON

May I see the back, please?

Mr Fischer holds up a hand mirror so Gordon can see the back. Gordon nods. Max comes in rolling a Japanese ten-speed at his side.

MR FISCHER

Hey, Max. How was your day?

MAX

Hm. I'd say

(*thinks for a second*)

Ninety-eight percent good, two percent not so good. I need a signature on this geometry test, by the way.

Max leaves his test on the counter and rolls his bike into the back room. Gordon gives Mr Fischer ten dollars.

GORDON

Thank you very much.

Gordon goes out the door. Mr Fischer looks at the geometry test. Max comes out of the back room drinking a glass of chocolate milk with a straw.

MR FISCHER

Hm.

MAX

I know.

MR FISCHER

A 37.

MAX

Pathetic. Just pathetic.

MR FISCHER

Well. It could've been worse. You were right more than a third of the time.

MAX
(*exploding*)

Come on, Dad! That stinks! I can do better than that!

MR FISCHER

Of course, you can.

MAX

For once, will you please try not to look on the bright side?

MR FISCHER

Sit down and let me give you a trim.

Max sighs deeply. He sits down. Mr Fischer signs the geometry test. He puts a pale-blue smock over Max and gives him a haircut.

MAX

Do you think I'm stupid?

MR FISCHER

No! You're just not very good at math.

MAX

But I'm failing English and History, too.

MR FISCHER
(*pause*)

Well. Maybe you'd be better off at a school where there's not so much emphasis on academics.

MAX

What, like barber college?

Mr Fisher is stricken. Max says quietly:

No. I love Rushmore. I don't want to go someplace second rate. Besides, it would ruin my chances of getting into Oxford.

Silence. Mr Fischer looks very sad.

MR FISCHER

I wish I knew how to help you. But I just don't. I'm sorry,
Max.

Max looks at his dad. Mr Fischer looks down at the floor.

You want to see the back?

MAX

No, thanks. You know how I like it.

INT. THE FISCHERS' HOUSE – NIGHT

*An Archie Bunker-type house. Max is cooking some spaghetti while Mr
Fischer sits at the kitchen table.*

MAX

You think I'm spending too much of my time starting up
clubs and putting on plays?

MR FISCHER

I don't know. It's possible.

MAX

I should probably be trying harder to score chicks. That's the
only thing anybody really cares about.
            (*sighs deeply*)
But it's not my forte, unfortunately.

21

MR FISCHER

It'll happen, Max. It's just. You're like one of those clipper ship captains. You're married to the sea.

MAX

Yes. That's true.
(*pause*)
But I've been out at sea for a long time.

EXT. SOCCER FIELD – DAY

Miss Cross is sitting on the bleachers watching her class play Capture-the-Flag. She opens a book. It is 20,000 Leagues under the Sea. *She puts a cigarette in her mouth and searches in her pocket for a lighter.*

A lit match appears in front of her. Max is holding it. He is wearing a maroon beret. Miss Cross looks at him curiously.

MAX

Hello.

MISS CROSS

Hi.

Miss Cross lights her cigarette from Max's match.

I like your hat.

MAX

Thank you. You're a teacher here, aren't you?

MISS CROSS

Uh-huh.

MAX

What subject do you teach?

MISS CROSS

Well, I teach first grade, so I do all the subjects. Except music.

MAX

And this is your first year at Rushmore, I take it.

Miss Cross nods.

I see. How long have you been a smoker, if you don't mind me asking?

                    MISS CROSS
Hm. Let's see. How old are you?

                    MAX
Fifteen.

                    MISS CROSS
Since I was your age.

                    MAX
                    (*shocked*)
You're kidding.

Miss Cross shakes her head. Max can't believe this.

You should quit.

                    MISS CROSS
You're right.

                    MAX
                    (*going back to his book*)
And I should mind my own business.

Miss Cross laughs. Max looks back up.

Where'd you go to school, by the way?

MISS CROSS

Harvard.

MAX

Really? That's a coincidence. My top schools where I want to apply are Oxford and the Sorbonne. But my safety is Harvard.

MISS CROSS
(*smiles*)

That's very ambitious.

MAX

Thank you.

MISS CROSS

What are you going to major in?

MAX

Well. I haven't decided for sure. But probably a double-major in Mathematics and Pre-Med. What was your major?

MISS CROSS

Latin-American studies.

MAX

Ah. That's interesting. Did you hear they're not going to teach Latin here anymore?

MISS CROSS

This is more like Central America.

MAX
(*pause*)

Sure. Central America and what-not. But moving on: they're going to cancel Latin. They have to make room for Japanese.

MISS CROSS

Really? That's too bad. All the Romance Languages come from Latin.

MAX

They do, don't they?

(*pause*)

24

Like French, probably.

She nods. She smiles.

> MISS CROSS
>
> *Nihilo sanctum estne?*

> MAX
>
> That's Latin, isn't it?

> MISS CROSS
>
> Yeah.

> MAX
>
> What does it mean?

> MISS CROSS
>
> Is nothing sacred?

Long pause. Looking right at her.

> MAX
>
> *Sic transit gloria.* Glory fades. I'm Max Fischer.

Max slides down the bench and puts out his hand.

> MISS CROSS
>
> Hi.

They shake hands.

INT. LUNCHROOM – DAY

A crowd of Middle Schoolers has gathered around Max. He is holding a clipboard. One of the kids finishes signing a piece of paper on it.

> MAX
>
> Good. Now you.
> > (*points to the next kid*)
>
> Sign here.

The kid signs.

INSERT PIECE OF PAPER:

A long list of signatures. Many of them are written in little kids' handwriting. Some are neater. Across the top it says PETITION. This is written in calligraphy.

CUT TO:

The administration conference room. Ten teachers sit in chairs around a long table. Max stands before them finishing a speech. The petition is tacked up on the wall behind him.

> MAX
> In summation I have only one question: is Latin dead? *Nisilum sacnus*
> > *(pause, looks at his notecards)*
> *estne?* Only you can say. Thank you for your time.

Applause.

INSERT ANNOUNCEMENT:

> Thanks in part to the efforts of tenth-class member Max Fischer, Latin will now be a required course for grades 7 through

INT. HALLWAY – DAY

Max and a bunch of other kids are reading this announcement on the bulletin board. Max is smiling serenely. The others are cursing and looking at Max with angry faces. Magnus Buchan is one of them. He has a strong Scottish accent.

> MAGNUS
> Bugger off, Fischer. Ya bleedin' little bollocks.

> MAX
> Is that Latin? Not bad, Buchan. Maybe you'll place out of your first year.

INT. GYM – DAY

Mr Blume's son Ronny is in a wrestling match. He has his opponent in a choke hold and is slowly strangling him. Mr Blume looks on distastefully from the stands. Max is at his side.

MR BLUME

What does your dad do, Max?

MAX
(*frankly*)

He's a neurosurgeon. Over at St Joseph's. Personally, I could never see myself cutting open somebody's brain. But he seems to enjoy it.

Max shrugs. Mr Blume nods.

You were in Vietnam, if I'm not mistaken, weren't you?

Mr Blume nods. Max thinks for a minute.

Were you in the shit?

MR BLUME

Yeah. I was in the shit.

They look back out at the wrestling match. Ronny is crushing his opponent's face into the mat with his fist. Mr Blume shakes his head.

Tell me something, Max. What do you think of Ronny and Donny?

MAX
(*automatically*)

I like them.

MR BLUME
(*surprised*)

Really?

MAX

Sure.

Ronny flips his opponent on the mat and flattens him with his body. Donny screams encouragement.

MR BLUME

No. You're right. They're good kids.

Max nods solemnly.

WRESTLER

See you Sunday, Mr Blume.

A stocky Wrestler with an ice pack on his arm walks by on his way to the showers. Mr Blume nods to him without looking up.

MAX

What's Sunday?

Mr Blume looks to Max. Silence.

MR BLUME

The twins are having a birthday party. And I'd love it if –

MAX

Oh, that's right. Yeah. I'm not going to be able to make it to that one.

Max smiles very sincerely. Silence.

MR BLUME

Come work for me.

MAX
(*stiffens*)

What do you mean?

MR BLUME

I mean, I could use somebody like you. I could –

MAX

I may not be rich, Mr Blume. And my father may only be a doctor. But we manage.

MR BLUME
(*hesitates*)

I didn't mean it like that. I just –

MAX

No, thank you. I mean, I appreciate the offer. But I've got everything I need right here at Rushmore. Besides, it wouldn't be fair.

REFEREE

110s!

MAX

Excuse me, Mr Blume. Nice talking with you.

Max pulls off his blazer. He is wearing wrestling tights underneath. Mr Blume looks surprised.

MR BLUME

You're on the team?

MAX
(*shrugs*)

I'm an alternate.

Max heads out to the mat, pulling on his headgear. Mr Blume calls after him:

MR BLUME

What wouldn't be fair, Max?

MAX
(*smiles crookedly*)

We'd make too much money working on the same team.

Mr Blume smiles faintly. He watches as Max begins his match. Max is clearly outclassed and quickly gets pinned.

INT. HALLWAY – DAY

Miss Cross is shepherding her class into her classroom. They are singing a song as they walk down the corridor. Across the hall a fourth-grade teacher, Mrs Guggenheim, comes out of her classroom. She is a handsome woman in her late sixties with black and silver hair.

MISS CROSS

Hello, Mrs Guggenheim.

MRS GUGGENHEIM

Hi, Rosemary. Did you find a place?

MISS CROSS

Well, I'm just staying over at Edward's parents' house for now. They're out of town.

MRS GUGGENHEIM

Oh. That's good.

(*pause*)
Edward was one of my students, you know.

Miss Cross smiles and nods. Silence. Miss Cross points to a photograph in a collage on the wall.

MISS CROSS
I think I met that boy yesterday.

Mrs Guggenheim looks at the picture.

INSERT PHOTOGRAPH:

It is a black and white of Max in fifth grade singing a show tune. His arms are opened wide and he has a top hat in one hand and a cane in the other.

MRS GUGGENHEIM
(*frowns*)
That's Max Fischer. How'd you get mixed up with him?

MISS CROSS
He introduced himself to me. I liked him, actually.

MRS GUGGENHIEM
(*resigned*)
Yeah, I know. So do I.

EXT. COUNTRY CLUB – DAY

Ronny and Donny set upon a pile of birthday presents at a table by the pool. They are surrounded by kids in swimsuits.

Mr Blume sits alone at the next table drinking a whiskey in front of the demolished birthday cake. He has a tattoo on his shoulder that says Semper Fi. There is a bucket of golf balls in front of him and he absently tosses them into the pool one at a time.

He looks over at Mrs Blume. She has red hair just like the twins. She is flirting with a pretty-boy Tennis Pro. She looks back to Mr Blume coldly.

Mr Blume gets up and walks around the pool. He pauses to shake hands with a Big Man drinking a glass of Scotch. The big man gives Mr Blume a sudden shove toward the pool, but hangs on to him so he doesn't fall in. The big man laughs.

Mr Blume climbs up the ladder to the high dive. He sets down his cocktail. He slips and falls and bangs his knee hard on the edge of the board. He gets up quickly. There is a bad cut on his knee and he is bleeding. He looks out at the birthday party down below.

People begin to notice him up there.

He sprints down the board, bounces once as high as he can, and sails out long through the air. He tucks into a cannon-ball. He nails the water with a huge splash.

Mrs Blume gets up with a bitter look on her face and heads for the ladies' room.

Kids gather at the edge of the pool to look down at Mr Blume playing dead at the bottom with golf balls all around him. A little boy in a Speedo swims underwater to examine Mr Blume. Their eyes meet. The boy turns and swims away.

INT. CLASSROOM — DAY

Miss Cross's classroom. The walls are lined with fishtanks that glow blue and make bubbling sounds. There are maps and pictures everywhere. A model of a 747 hangs from the ceiling. A record player plays the Vienna Boys' Choir at a low volume.

There is only one Kid in the room. He is taking a test. Miss Cross sits at her desk grading papers.

Max cracks open the door.

MAX

Miss Cross?

Miss Cross and the kid look back at Max. Miss Cross holds her finger to her lips and gets up. As she walks past the kid she puts her hand on the top of his head. She goes to Max at the door. She whispers:

MISS CROSS

He's taking a make-up test.

MAX

These guys have tests?

MISS CROSS

Of course.

MAX

I thought they just did coloring and stuff.

MISS CROSS

Oh, no. They're good readers.

MAX

I'm Max Fischer. We met the other day.

MISS CROSS

I know who you are. How are you?

MAX

Fine, thank you.

Max just stands there.

MISS CROSS

You want to help me feed the fish?

MAX

Yes, please.

Max follows her from tank to tank as she shakes out fish food. They continue to whisper to each other:

I thought I would just let you know, as per our conversation the other day –

MISS CROSS

Latin?

MAX

Right. The Romance Languages. I gave a little speech –

MISS CROSS

I heard about this.

MAX

You did?

MISS CROSS

Uh-huh. I understand you made a very convincing argument.

MAX

I thought you'd be pleased to hear they're going to continue the Latin program.

She looks at Max. She sets down the fish food and shakes his hand.

MISS CROSS

I'm very impressed.

MAX

Thank you very much.

Max picks up the can of fish food and shakes some into one of the aquariums.

You need an assistant?

MISS CROSS
(*smiles*)

Do we get to have assistants around here?

MAX

I doubt it. I'm on scholarship, though. Academic scholarship. So sometimes I get to do odd jobs.
(*pause*)
How did you decide to teach at Rushmore?

MISS CROSS

My husband went here.

Max drops the can of fish food into the tank. He quickly fishes it out.

He picks some little bits of fish food out of the water and throws them away. Pause.

MAX

I didn't know you were married.

MISS CROSS

Well, he's dead now. So I'm not, actually.

MAX

When did he die?

MISS CROSS

Last year.

Max nods. Silence.

MAX

My mother's dead.

MISS CROSS

Oh. I'm sorry to hear that.

MAX

She died when I was seven.
(*raising an eyebrow*)
So we both have dead people in our families.

They look at each other for a minute.

Now what's going on in here?

Max kneels down and looks into one of the fishtanks. There are a hundred little seahorses swimming around in it.

MISS CROSS

Those were just born.

A look of wonder comes across Max's face. He stares into the blue water.

MAX

You really love fish, don't you?

Miss Cross nods. Max puts his fingers to the glass.

How much do these cost?

INT. BLUME INTERNATIONAL CONCRETE – DAY

Mr Blume's office. He is talking on the telephone. Max sits in a chair across from him.

> MR BLUME
> I don't want any alloys. I want steel.
>> *(pause)*
> I don't give a rat's ass if he did.
>> *(pause)*
> Steel, Harry.

He hangs up.

You change your mind? You want the job?

> MAX
> No. But I've got an idea. And I need some money.

Mr Blume's secretary buzzes him on the speakerphone.

> SECRETARY
> Mr Blume, they're ready for you in Hydraulics.

> MR BLUME
> Come with me. Let's hear your idea.

INT. FACTORY – DAY

Max, Mr Blume, and a big foreman named Ernie race across the factory in a souped-up golf cart. They're squeezed together with Max in the middle.

> MAX
> Rushmore deserves an aquarium. A first class aquarium where scientists can lecture, and students can study marine life in their natural –

> MR BLUME
> I don't know. What do you think, Ernie?

                        ERNIE
                      (*skeptical*)
An aquarium?

                         MAX
A huge aquarium. An entire building.

                        ERNIE
What kind of fish?

INT. FACTORY – DAY

*Mr Blume and Max, wearing hard hats, stand on scaffolding
overlooking a huge vat of bubbling concrete.*

                         MAX
                      (*shouting*)
Electric eels. Barracudas. Stingrays. Hammerheads. Piranhas.

                     MR BLUME
Piranhas?

                         MAX
That's right. Piranhas. I talked to a man in South America.

                     MR BLUME
Really. So you might have piranhas.

                         MAX
We *will* have piranhas.

INT. MR BLUME'S OFFICE – DAY

Back in Mr Blume's office. They're seated as before. Max is still wearing his hard hat.

MR BLUME

What does Guggenheim say?

MAX

Nothing. I felt I should go to you first.

MR BLUME

Why?

MAX

Because at this moment I feel our best strategy is to keep a low profile. The more preparation I can do, the stronger our case will be when we go to the administration.

Long pause.

MR BLUME

How much do you want?

MAX

$35,000 for the initial plans.

Max holds Mr Blume's gaze. Mr Blume picks up a pen.

MR BLUME

I'll give you $2500.

Max nods. Mr Blume writes out a check, tears it off, and hands it to Max. Max sticks it in his pocket like it is a five dollar bill.

RESEARCH MONTAGE:

All of the following events occur during school hours.

Max strides across the quadrangle with a determined expression. He's got an armload of books on marine life.

Max watches a Jacques Cousteau film on 16mm in an empty classroom. Dirk runs the projector.

Max visits a marine research facility and talks with a Scientist. Max holds up a fish at the edge of a pool. A killer whale jumps out of the water and takes it in its teeth.

Max flies over Rushmore in a chopper with Mr Blume. He shouts out details of the landscape and Mr Blume nods enthusiastically. They are both eating sandwiches.

They set down on the soccer field. Kids come running out to meet them. Max waves to them as he jumps out of the chopper. He looks back to Mr Blume and gives him a thumbs-up. Mr Blume smiles and waves as the chopper takes off.

Max walks with a young Architect among the trees between the gym and the baseball diamond. They look at some blueprints. Max pulls up third base and slides it over a few feet.

Max points to some beautiful fish in an aquarium in a pet shop. The pet shop Owner reaches in with a little net.

Max pokes his head into Miss Cross's classroom. He holds up two plastic baggies full of water with tropical fish swimming around inside them.

Kids gather all around them as they put the new fish into the aquariums. Max smiles mysteriously.

MAX
You need any help grading papers or anything?

INSERT BOOK REPORT:

The title is 'Young Ben Franklin'. Miss Cross writes Magnificent! Keep up the good work! and draws two stars across the top of the page with a red pen.

INT. MISS CROSS'S CLASSROOM – DAY

Max is staring at Miss Cross in a trance from a desk opposite hers in the empty classroom. She looks up at him. He continues to stare at her as if she were a statue.

Miss Cross rubs her eyes and sighs. She sets down her red pen. She looks back to Max. He is still staring at her.

Max?

Max looks quickly down to his papers.

MAX

Uh-huh?

MISS CROSS

Can I ask you something?

MAX

Sure.

MISS CROSS

Has it ever crossed your mind that you're way too young for
me?

Max looks up. Miss Cross smiles faintly. Silence.

MAX

It's crossed my mind that you might consider that a
possibility, yes.

MISS CROSS

Not to mention that you're a student –

MAX

And you're a teacher. And never the twain shall meet. I know.
I'm not trying to pressure you into anything, Miss Cross. I'm
surprised you brought it up so bluntly.

MISS CROSS

I just want to make sure –

MAX

We've become friends, haven't we?

MISS CROSS

Yes.

MAX

Good. That's all that matters to me.

Max thinks for a second, then presses on:

And the truth is neither one of us has the slightest idea where this relationship is going. We can't predict the future.

> MISS CROSS
>
> We don't have a relationship, Max.

> MAX
>
> But we're friends.

> MISS CROSS
>
> Yes. And that's all we're going to be.

> MAX
>
> That's what I meant by relationship. You want me to grab a dictionary?

> MISS CROSS
>
> I just want to make sure we understand each other.

> MAX
>
> I understand. You're not attracted to me. *C'est la vie.* I'm a big boy.

> MISS CROSS
>
> Max. You're fifteen. Attraction doesn't enter into it.

> MAX
>
> If you say so. All I'm getting at is I've never met anyone like you. Take that for whatever it's worth.

She thinks about this for a minute.

> MISS CROSS
>
> I think I can safely say I've never met anyone like you, either.

> MAX
>
> You haven't, have you?

Miss Cross shakes her head. Max says quietly:

You want to shake hands?

She puts out her hand and they shake hands across the desk. But they don't let go. They just look at each other.

I'm glad we had this conversation.

Frank wheels around and knocks the clipboard out of O'Reilly's hands. He grabs O'Reilly by both arms. Fields instinctively draws his firearm.

FRANK

Promise me one thing, O'Reilly. You're going to follow this all the way. To the end
> (*snaps*)

of the line,
> (*snaps*)

where I got to be.

O'REILLY
> (*looking Frank right in the eye*)

So help me, God.

The audience is deeply engrossed. A row of small kids are sitting on the floor at the very front.

Max watches from the wings. He looks out at the audience.

He sees Mr Blume smiling proudly in the third row.

He sees Miss Cross sitting next to a big, curly-haired Medical Student in surgical scrubs. She leans close to him and whispers something in his ear. He smiles and nods and whispers something back.

Max stares at them blankly as a shootout erupts onstage.

INT. BACKSTAGE – NIGHT

Frank comes offstage with a bandage on his cheek and a cane in his hand. Max is waiting for him backstage. Max has on a headset and carries a clipboard. He is extremely keyed-up.

MAX

What happened to the cannoli line?

Max follows Frank as Frank walks quickly toward the dressing rooms.

You're supposed to say, Forget about it, Sanchez –

FRANK
> (*very angry*)

I made a mistake, all right? It didn't make any difference, anyway.

MAX

Hey, I'm letting it go. But don't tell me it doesn't matter. Every line matters.

FRANK
(*yelling*)

Get off my back!

MAX

Don't fuck with my play!

Frank turns around and punches Max in the nose. Max takes a swing and misses and they wrestle around as people try to break it up.

INT. AUDITORIUM — NIGHT

The whole cast is onstage bowing as the audience applauds. Some of the actors motion to the wings.

Max walks out on to the stage. He has a bloody Kleenex in each nostril. He waves to the audience. The applause roars.

INT. BACKSTAGE — NIGHT

The crowded dressing rooms. Actors are taking off their make-up. Max is drinking a champagne cocktail and talking with his father and an elderly Woman.

WOMAN

I thought the acting tonight was excellent.

MAX

It was better in rehearsals
(*to his father*)
I'll catch up with you later, Dad. I've got a dinner to go to.

MR FISCHER
(*interested*)

Oh, yeah?

MAX
(*pause*)

Yeah. Cast and crew only.

Mr Fischer feels left out but tries not to show it.

MR FISCHER

OK. Well, have a good time.

Miss Cross walks over to Max through the crowd. Her friend the medical student follows behind her. Max's expression is polite but inscrutable.

MISS CROSS

That was great, Max.

MAX

I'm so glad you could come.

MISS CROSS

I want you to meet a friend of mine. John Coats. Max Fischer.

MAX
(*not looking at him*)

Who's this guy?

MISS CROSS
(*pause*)

John.

Max looks at John. John smiles. Pause.

44

                    JOHN
I really liked your play, man. It was really cool.

Max nods. He drinks a long sip of his champagne cocktail.

                MISS CROSS
What happened to your nose?

                    MAX
I got punched in the face.
                (*to John*)
What's your excuse?

Mr Blume comes over to them.

                MR BLUME
Am I going to get to meet your dad tonight, Max?

                    MAX
Nah. The old man's on call tonight. Mr Blume, I'd like you
to meet Miss Cross, and I didn't catch this young
gentleman's name.

INT. RESTAURANT – NIGHT

*A fancy restaurant. Max is having dinner with Mr Blume, Miss Cross
and John. Max is drunk.*

                    MAX
I like your nurse's uniform, guy.

                    JOHN
These are OR scrubs.

                    MAX
                (*pause*)
OR they?

*Mr Blume laughs suddenly and wine goes up his nose. Max glances to
him slyly, then looks back to John.*

Well, they're totally inappropriate for the occasion.

                    JOHN
Well, I didn't know we were going to dinner.

45

MAX

That's because you weren't invited.

MR BLUME

Take it easy, Max.

MISS CROSS
(*angry*)

You're the one who ordered him a Scotch and soda.

MAX

What's wrong with that? I can write a hit play. Why can't I
have a drink when I want to unwind a little? So tell me,
Curly. How do you know Miss Cross?

JOHN

We went to Harvard together.

MAX
(*shrugs*)

And I wrote a hit play. And directed it. So I'm not sweating
it, either.

MR BLUME
(*signaling the waiter*)

I'm going to get the check.

MAX

What do you think you're doing?

MR BLUME

I'm getting the –

MAX

No, you're not.

The Waiter comes over. Max intercepts him:

I just wanted to thank you again for accommodating us. We only expected to be a party of three, but somebody invited himself along. I apologize.

WAITER

That's perfectly all right.

The waiter walks away. Miss Cross frowns.

MISS CROSS

You're being rude, Max.

MAX

No, I'm not. I'm just trying to figure out why you brought this gentleman to my play. And my dinner, which was invitation only.

John reaches in front of Max for the butter. Max grabs his spoon and swats John on the back of the hand.

Would you like me to pass you the butter?

Max hands John the butter.

MISS CROSS

What's wrong with you?

MAX
(*raising his voice*)

What's wrong with *you*?

Max is making a scene. People all over the restaurant are watching. Max stares at Miss Cross.

You hurt my feelings. This night was important to me.

MISS CROSS

How did I hurt your feelings?

I wrote a hit play!

(pause)

And I'm in love with you.

John looks to Miss Cross. She doesn't know what to say. Max looks drunk and dejected.

How do you like that, Curly?

EXT. PLAYGROUND – DAY

Miss Cross and her pupils are out on the playground painting pictures. Each kid has an easel.

Miss Cross sees Mr Blume standing under a tree at the edge of the playground. He is wearing sunglasses and smoking a cigarette. He moves slightly behind the tree. She stares at him.

He waves. She waves back. He comes over.

MR BLUME

Hi.

MISS CROSS

Were you hiding over there?

Mr Blume shrugs. He points at one of the paintings.

MR BLUME

What's that?

The Artist looks up at Mr Blume. He is a small boy with jet-black curly hair and piercing eyes.

ARTIST
(*makes a swimming gesture*)
It's a little swimming snake.

Mr Blume nods.

MISS CROSS

What can I do for you, Mr Blume?

Mr Blume turns to Miss Cross and takes off his sunglasses. Silence.

MR BLUME

Max wants to see you.

MISS CROSS

What for?

MR BLUME

To apologize, I guess.

MISS CROSS

He sent you here?

MR BLUME

Yeah.

She frowns and studies Mr Blume for a minute.

MISS CROSS

Are you his messenger?

MR BLUME

No. He's my friend.
(*pause*)
You were right. I shouldn't have let him drink.

Miss Cross nods. Silence.

MISS CROSS

I don't think I should see Max any more.

49

He's not going to like the sound of that.

MISS CROSS
I know. But I think I let him get too attached.

Mr Blume nods. Miss Cross looks uncertain.

Don't you think?

MR BLUME
(*shrugs*)
I don't know. You did your best.

Miss Cross smiles sadly to Mr Blume. He puts his hands in his pockets.

MISS CROSS
Tell him I'm sorry.

MR BLUME
OK.

They look at each other for a long minute. Miss Cross tucks a strand of hair behind her ear. Mr Blume says quietly:

What's your first name?

MISS CROSS
Rosemary. What's yours?

MR BLUME
Herman.

Silence.

Oh, yeah. He wrote you a letter.

He hands her a letter in a sealed envelope. She takes it.

MISS CROSS
Thanks.

They stand there in silence for another minute.

MR BLUME
OK. So long, Rosemary.

                    MISS CROSS
                     (*smiles*)
Bye, Herman.

Mr Blume starts to go. He stops. He looks back to Miss Cross.

                    MR BLUME
Should we meet somewhere?

She hesitates.

To talk about Max.

                    MISS CROSS
Yeah. I don't know.
                     (*pause*)
Maybe.

*Mr Blume nods. He turns away and walks off. She watches him go.
She looks at the envelope.*

INSERT LETTER WRITTEN IN CALLIGRAPHY ON CRISP
STATIONERY:

Max reads in voice-over.

Dear Miss Cross,
    I would like to take this opportunity to formally
apologize for the events of the night of the twenty-third.
I am not accustomed to drinking alcohol. Please do me
the service of coming to the unveiling of a new venture
I have undertaken. I hope you will attend, if possible. I
remain, your friend,
                                        Max Fischer

EXT. VACANT LOT – DAY

*A crowd of fifty Kids in uniform has gathered around the vacant lot
beside the baseball field. Max stands with his architect, smiling for the
yearbook photographer. They are holding a banner that says
'Cousteau–Blume Marine Observatory Fundraiser'. Max has on a
hard hat. There are two pick-up trucks and a porta-can at the back of
the vacant lot.*

Max digs into the ground with a gold shovel. The shovel has a ribbon around it. Flashbulbs go off. Everyone claps. Max waves Dirk over.

> MAX

Did you see her?

> DIRK

She's not here.

> MAX

Well, see if she's in her classroom.

The Contractor walks over to Max.

> CONTRACTOR

Should we go ahead and take care of this tree?

> MAX

Let's wait a few minutes.

Coach Beck goes over to Max. He is six four and wears a John Newcombe moustache and an Adidas warm-up. He is frowning.

> COACH BECK

What's going on here, Maxie?

> MAX

Coach Beck. Good to see you. This is where they're building the new aquarium. I'm in charge of the committee, if you can believe it.

> COACH BECK

This is the baseball diamond.

> MAX

I believe it's being relocated a few feet over.

> COACH BECK
> *(frowns)*

I should've been informed about that.

Coach Beck walks off. Max answers some questions for the School Reporters.

> REPORTER

Is it true the aquarium will have piranhas?

                              MAX
                          (*smiles*)
Where'd you hear that?

                            REPORTER
My source indicated that it was a possibility.

                              MAX
Yes, it's true. Excuse me, George.

Dirk has returned.

What's the story?

                             DIRK
                       (*a little wary*)
She has a substitute teacher today.

                              MAX
Why?

                             DIRK
She probably got sick.

                              MAX
                         (*looks away*)
You know she's not sick. Give me the phone.

Max dials on a cellular phone.

Hi, Janet. It's Max Fischer. Is Mr Blume there?
                          (*pause*)
Well, where is he?
                          (*pause*)
Goddammit, he's supposed to be here. Let me know if you
find him, please.

Max hangs up. He looks off and says in a steely voice:

I'm going anyway.

Max goes over to the contractor:

Chop it down, Mr Chandler! We've got an aquarium to
build.

                               53

Max talks to another reporter.

I don't give a shit about barracudas. But fuck it. I'm building it anyway.

The sound of power saws fills the air as Dr Guggenheim appears at the edge of the lot with Coach Beck and a Security Guard with a walkie-talkie. Dr Guggenheim screams:

DR GUGGENHEIM
Max!

Dr Guggenheim sees the chopped-down trees and mangled baseball field as he strides on to the lot.

MAX
Nice to see you, Dr Gugg –

DR GUGGENHEIM
Max!
(*seizing Max by the arm*)
What do you think you're doing?

MAX
(*pause*)
We're having a fundraiser for –

DR GUGGENHEIM
Shut those damn things off!

They turn off the power saws.

Tell me this isn't happening.

                    MAX
Dr Guggenheim, I'd rather not have this conversation in front
of the crew.

EXT. QUADRANGLE – DAY

*Dirk waits nervously on the steps in front of Dr Guggenheim's office. He
holds a hamster in his hands.*

He gets up and goes to the window. He looks inside.

*Max is sitting in a little chair in the middle of the room with his hard
hat on. Dr Guggenheim and several other faculty members sit around
him. Dr Guggenheim is screaming at him across his desk. Max is
crying.*

Dirk looks scared.

INT. HALLWAY – DAY

*Max kneels on the floor in the hallway, emptying out his locker. Papers
and trash are scattered all around him. There is a trashcan beside him.
He is throwing away his books, one at a time.*

*Mr Blume opens the door at the end of the hallway. Max looks up at
him. Silence. Max looks back to his locker and starts throwing his books
in the trash again.*

*Mr Blume walks over to Max. He looks very sad. He kneels down
beside Max. He starts helping him pick up the trash off the floor and
put it in the trashcan.*

TITLE:

                  October

INT. GROVER CLEVELAND HIGH SCHOOL – DAY

*Grover Cleveland is a public high school with two thousand five
hundred students.*

Max sits in the front row of a math classroom. He is dressed in his Rushmore uniform, with coat and tie, but his clothes are wrinkled and his head has been shaved like a marine's. His eyes have dark circles around them. He has a little stack of index cards in his hand.

The teacher, Mrs Whitney, stands at the front of the room. She is about fifty with horn-rimmed glasses and a slight English accent. She has a bemused expression on her face.

> MRS WHITNEY
> We have a new student with us today. His name's Max Fischer and he's actually asked to say a few words to the class. Max? You want to take it away?

> MAX
> (*standing up*)
> Sure. Thanks very much. I just wanted to introduce myself.

Max looks quickly at his notecards.

> I'm Max Fischer. I'm a former student of Rushmore Academy, which I recently got expelled from.

Max flips to the next notecard.

> This is my first time in a public school. And I know you probably think I was born with a silver spoon in my mouth. But I'm no elitist. I think you've got some great facilities, and I'm really looking forward to making the best of it over here at Grover Cleveland.

Max sighs deeply. He rubs his eyes. His Classmates have no idea what to make of him. However, one Asian girl in the back row is smiling faintly. She has short-cropped hair. The spine of one of her bookcovers says Margaret Yang.

> One footnote: I noticed you don't have a fencing team. I'm going to start one up. Let me know if you'd like to join. Thanks.

INT. GROVER CLEVELAND HIGH SCHOOL – DAY

The wide halls of Grover Cleveland High are lined with orange lockers. A banner stretched down the wall says 'Murder the Mustangs'. A bustling throng of high schoolers rushes to class.

Max walks slowly, alone, down the middle of the hall. A blonde cheerleader-type Girl asks him:

GIRL

Why are you so dressed up?

Max looks down at his clothes. He looks back to the girl.

MAX

Are you insane?

The girl walks off. Margaret Yang catches up to Max.

MARGARET

Max?

MAX
(*frowns*)

Yes?

MARGARET

Hi. I'm Margaret Yang. I'm in Mrs Whitney's class. I just wanted to tell you I liked your speech. I don't think I've ever heard of anyone asking to give a speech in class before.

MAX

How unfortunate.

MARGARET

The silver spoon remark might rub some people the wrong way. But I think I know how you meant it.

MAX

Glad to hear it. Goodbye, Miss Chang.

Max ducks into the men's room. Margaret walks quietly away.

INT. GYMNASIUM – DAY

A tiny figure dressed all in white stands alone at the far end of the huge gymnasium with a fencing foil. He lunges, parries, thrusts.

The basketball team suddenly floods dribbling into the gymnasium, throwing passes and taking free throws. Max stops fencing as they take over the room. He watches them in silence. He shakes his head. He walks off the court.

INT. HALLWAY – DAY

Max puts a quarter in a pay phone. He is still wearing his fencing costume.

> MAX
>
> Janet. Max Fischer. Is he in?

EXT. RUSHMORE – DAY

Mr Blume answers on his cellular phone as he gets out of his car and walks across the lawn at Rushmore.

We intercut the two of them.

> MR BLUME
>
> Hey, Max. How's it going over there?

> MAX
>
> Terrible. Tell me something. When you talked to Miss Cross the other day, did you get the feeling –

The hall monitor Mr Holstead comes down the hall toward Max. He is a big, sturdy man about fifty years old. He wears a striped tie and his sleeves rolled up.

> MR HOLSTEAD
> (*loudly*)
>
> Do you have a telephone pass?

Max holds up his hand for Mr Holstead to wait a minute. He covers his ear so he can hear Mr Blume.

Mr Blume is looking in the windows of different classrooms. Kids look out at him curiously.

> MR BLUME
>
> I got to tell you, Max. I don't know what you see in her. I don't think she's right for you.

> MAX
>
> What's that supposed to mean?

58

Mr Blume sees Miss Cross inside teaching her class. He stares at her in a trance. He whispers:

> MR BLUME
>
> Well, she's not *that* beautiful. She's not *that* interesting. I mean, sure, there's something about her. But I see you with someone –

> MAX
>
> Look, Mr Blume. You comments are valuable, but let's get to the point. Will she see me again? Yes or no?

> MR BLUME
> (*pause*)

No.

> MAX
>
> I'm going to go see her. Hang on.

Max looks to Mr Holstead.

> I'm talking on the telephone.

Mr Holstead reaches over and hangs up the phone.

> Come on, man. That's rude.

INT. GROVER CLEVELAND HIGH SCHOOL – DAY

Mrs Whitney watches from her classroom window as:

Max opens a red metal door on to the empty concrete courtyard. He looks left and right. He sneaks across the courtyard to the bike racks, quickly unlocks his bike, and rides away.

EXT. RUSHMORE – DAY

Max rides full speed through the gates on to the Rushmore campus. He flips one leg off his bike and glides in toward the bike racks standing on one pedal.

Max locks up his bike and walks across the lawn.

> MAGNUS
>
> You better beat it, laddie.

Max looks up at Magnus Buchan sitting in a tree smoking a cigarette, hacking at a branch with a pocketknife.

> MAX
>
> I hope you fall out of that tree and get stuck in the ass, Buchan.

> MAGNUS
>
> You know, I've watched you, Fischer. Showboat, always talking, picking a kid like Dirk cause his mother's a great piece and then getting nowhere. Like everything you do. Big show. No results.

> MAX
>
> And what do you call getting a hand job from Mrs Calloway in her Jaguar?

> MAGNUS
>
> A bloody lie.

> MAX
>
> You think I got kicked out for just the aquarium? Nah. That ain't it. It was the hand job. And I'll tell you another thing. It was worth it. So eat your heart out out, mick. I got business to attend to.

EXT. PARKING LOT – DAY

Miss Cross comes out the door of the lower school with a basket of books and papers. She stops in front of her station wagon and digs in her bag for her keys.

MAX

I'm sorry I embarrassed you at dinner.

Miss Cross turns around. Max is standing across the driveway with a sad smile on his face. Silence.

MISS CROSS

That's OK.

MAX

No, it's not. And please apologize to what's his name for me.

MISS CROSS

I will. Are you OK?

MAX

I'm fine. But I miss Rushmore. I miss the seasons. And watching the leaves change.

MISS CROSS

But it's only three blocks away.

MAX

I know. And I miss seeing you.

MISS CROSS
(*pause*)

I miss you, too.

Max looks off into the trees. A squirrel leaps from one branch to another. Max smiles and shakes his head. A crashing noise is heard from the roof of the planetarium. Someone ducks for cover, but Max and Miss Cross do not see him.

Max reaches into his backpack and says mysteriously:

MAX

By the way. What time does the library close? I got an overdue book to turn in.

Max takes out the Jacques Cousteau library book and hands it to Miss

Cross. She looks at it and starts to say something, but she stops. She opens the book and looks at it in silence.

That's your handwriting, isn't it?

Max shows her the Jacques Cousteau quote. Miss Cross nods.

Not bad. Except it's probably bad form for a teacher to write in a library book.

MISS CROSS
It wasn't a library book when I wrote in it.

MAX
What do you mean?

MISS CROSS
I gave this book to Rushmore.

Max looks puzzled. Miss Cross shows him a little card inside the front cover of the book.

INSERT LIBRARY BOOK:

In Memory of EDWARD APPLEBY
Class of '87

My husband gave me this book in seventh grade. And he went to Rushmore. So when he died I put it in the library here.

MAX
So that's who that is. Edward Appleby.
                    (*looks to Miss Cross*)
You already knew him in seventh grade?

MISS CROSS
I knew him all my life.
                    (*looks to Max*)
You remind me of him, you know.

MAX
I do? How?

MISS CROSS
Well. Weren't you in the Rushmore Bee-keepers?

MAX
(*frowns*)
Yeah. I was president of them.

MISS CROSS
(*shrugs*)
He founded that club.

MAX
(*pause*)
I get your meaning. I founded a few clubs myself in my day.

An acorn falls on Max's head. He looks up. There is no one there, but a scurrying sound is heard. Max frowns.

What was that? A squirrel?

Mr Blume is crouched just out of view, on the roof. He looks back over his shoulder and sees a small, white-haired, Indian Groundskeeper looking at him. The groundskeeper is holding a rake. Mr Blume rises slowly. He whispers:

MR BLUME
Is this the natatorium?

The groundskeeper frowns and shakes his head.

MAX
Do you think we can be friends again, Miss Cross? In a strictly platonic way.

MISS CROSS
Of course, I do. Do you think you can make a go of it and settle down over at Grover Cleveland?

MAX
Yeah. But I need a tutor.

MISS CROSS
I'll be your tutor.

MAX
(*looking into her eyes*)
You will?

Miss Cross smiles and nods.

Thank you.
> (*pause*)

What are you doing tomorrow?

CUT TO:

Mr Blume sitting at the desk in his office. Max yells at him over the speakerphone:

She's taking me on a field trip!

> MR BLUME
> (*hesitates*)

Great! You need anybody to help you chaperone?

> MAX

You'd take the time out of your business to do that?

> MR BLUME

Business schmizness.

OCTOBER MONTAGE:

Max and Miss Cross ride in the backseat of a van full of first graders. Max is telling a story and everyone is laughing. Mr Blume is up front quietly driving the van. One of the first graders sits in the passenger seat staring at him. They go through the front gates of the zoo.

Miss Cross stands at the front of her classroom drawing a complicated geometric proof on the chalkboard. Max sits alone across from her nodding earnestly and taking notes.

Max and Miss Cross play doubles against Mr Blume and Dirk on the court in the Blume's backyard. Max coaches Miss Cross on her backhand. Mr Blume watches her from across the net. Mrs Blume watches all of them from an upstairs window.

The Grover Cleveland Science Fair. Max sits proudly in front of his project. It is a papier mâché tidal wave looming over a little coastal village with screaming peasants.

Margaret Yang is across the aisle being photographed with a trophy for Best of Show. Her project is called Back on Course: Global Convection,

Wind Systems, and the Subtropical Jet Stream. Several little model planes are on display. Margaret is staring at Max, but he does not notice her.

Mrs Whitney hands Max a geometry test. It has a C+ on it. Max looks quickly to Mrs Whitney, surprised. She smiles and shakes his hand.

A huge banner for the Grover Cleveland Owls is stretched across the endzone of the football field. Max, dressed in a shiny blue and grey jumpsuit, bursts through the banner and runs out on to the field doing cartwheels and flips. The football team scrambles out behind him.

Max points to different parts of the crowd and yells football cheers. Dirk is sitting in between Mr Blume and Miss Cross in the stands. Mr Blume stares at Miss Cross. Miss Cross looks back at Mr Blume and smiles. Dirk says significantly:

DIRK

Where's Mrs Blume tonight, Mr Blume? And your two sons Ronny and Donny.

MR BLUME
(*smiles*)

I have no idea, Dirk.

INT. GROVER CLEVELAND HIGH SCHOOL – DAY

Max bursts through a doorway followed by a little entourage of underclassmen that includes a sophomore named Woody. Woody has long hair and a Led Zeppelin T-shirt. He is carrying a clipboard.

They go down the hallway and walk quickly past Margaret Yang. She is dressed very nicely in a grey turtleneck.

> MARGARET

Hi, Max.

> MAX

Hi.

Max keeps walking.

He stops. He turns back to Margaret Yang. He looks her up and down. She is slightly uneasy. Max looks to Woody. Woody shrugs. Max looks back to Margaret.

What's your name again?

> MARGARET

Margaret Yang.

> MAX

Are you free seventh period?

> MARGARET

Well. I'm supposed to have guitar lessons.

> MAX
> (*pause*)

Classical?

> MARGARET

Rock.

> MAX

You can get out of it.
> (*to Woody*)

Put Margaret down for three-thirty in the auditorium, Woody.

Max turns away and walks briskly down the hall with his entourage. He calls back to Margaret:

And bring a headshot.

EXT. MISS CROSS'S HOUSE – DAY

A nice two story house with a wide lawn and lots of trees. Mr Blume knocks on the front door and waits nervously. He looks around the yard with his hands in his pockets.

The door opens. Miss Cross is holding a plate of sliced carrots. She looks at Mr Blume curiously and smiles.

> MISS CROSS
> Hi, Herman.

> MR BLUME
> How are you, Rosemary?

> MISS CROSS
> Fine, thanks. I just got home and I'm having a little snack.

> MR BLUME
> Having some carrots.

Miss Cross nods. Mr Blume looks up at the house.

Nice house.

> MISS CROSS
> Yeah. This isn't mine. I'm just kind of housesitting.
> *(pause)*
> Were you in the neighborhood?

Mr Blume nods. There is an awkward silence.

> MR BLUME
> Didn't Max have something planned for us today? A trip to the museum or something?

> MISS CROSS
> Did he? I thought he was rehearsing this evening.

> MR BLUME
> Oh. That's right. His new play. He's going to be in this one, isn't he?

Miss Cross nods. Mr Blume shakes his head.

He's really making a go of it over at Grover Cleveland.

MISS CROSS

I think he's on track. It's nice, isn't it?

Mr Blume nods. Silence.

You want a carrot?

MR BLUME

Yeah. I'll have one of those.

Mr Blume takes one of the carrots and has a bite of it. Miss Cross watches him chewing. She smiles slightly.

Well. Max had said something about us all going to the horse races, so I'm sure I'll see you soon.

Miss Cross nods. Mr Blume takes another bite of his carrot and throws the rest of it into the yard. Miss Cross laughs. Mr Blume smiles and shrugs. He starts to go.

MISS CROSS

Or we could go for a walk, if you want.

Mr Blume stops and turns around quickly.

MR BLUME

Sure.

MISS CROSS

It's nice out, don't you think? Kind of brisk.

Mr Blume nods.

Let me get a sweater. I'll be right back.

She goes inside. Mr Blume stands alone on the doorstep. He rubs his hands together to warm up.

INT. MUSEUM – DAY

A class of Rushmore Fourth Graders file past a big painting of a ship caught in a storm and disappear into the next room. One of them immediately comes back and looks around the corner. It is Dirk. He has seen something:

Miss Cross and Mr Blume are sitting on a bench in front of a

Rembrandt. They are holding hands.

Dirk narrows his eyes.

EXT. RUSHMORE – DAY

Mr Blume is parked at the curb, staring off into space. Ronny and Donny jump into the car and slam the doors.

                    RONNY
Let's go.

Mr Blume automatically puts the car in gear. He slams on the brakes. Dirk is standing in front of the car, blocking them. He stares at Mr Blume. Mr Blume rolls down his window.

                    MR BLUME
Dirk?

Dirk does not budge. Mr Blume gets out of the car and leaves it idling. He closes his door.

Dirk? What's wrong?

                    DIRK
I know about you and the teacher.

Silence. Mr Blume looks very worried.

                    MR BLUME
Does Max know?

                    DIRK
No. And I don't want him to know. Ever. I just want it to stop. Right now.

They stare at each other.

                    DIRK
You're a married man, Blume. And you're supposed to be his friend.

                    MR BLUME
Look, Dirk. I am his friend –

Yeah. And with friends like you, who needs friends?

Dirk turns and walks off. Mr Blume looks puzzled.

MR BLUME

Jesus Christ.

Mr Blume sighs. He turns around and tries to open his car door. Ronny and Donny have locked him out of the car. He can see them inside laughing. He says fiercely:

Unlock it!

CUT TO:

Dirk walking across the lawn with a hard look on his face. He walks past Magnus Buchan. Magnus is throwing Chinese throwing stars at a tree trunk.

MAGNUS

Little Calloway.

Dirk stops and looks to Magnus.

You're standing up for the wrong bloke. Fischer ain't your mate.

DIRK
(*angry*)

What are you talking about, Buchan?

MAGNUS
(*shrugs*)

He thinks your mum's good for a bonk. That's why he picked you for his chapel partner.

Dirk looks deeply wounded. But he doesn't want to believe it.

DIRK

Who sold you that crock?

MAGNUS

He told me himself. He says she gave him a hand job in the backseat of her bloody Jaguar.

DIRK

Max would never say that.

MAGNUS
(*smiles*)
Yeah. You're probably right. After all, the son of a brain
doctor doesn't need to impress anybody.

Buchan laughs wickedly and fires off another throwing star.

INT. GROVER CLEVELAND HIGH SCHOOL – NIGHT

*The school auditorium. Max is onstage dressed as a South Central
lowrider called Little Juan. He is opposite a senior named 40 Ounce and
Margaret Yang, who plays Blue Eyes. While they are rehearsing the
scene a Messenger comes in with an envelope for Max.*

LITTLE JUAN

The killing has got to stop, esse. It's getting too loco. No
more gats.

40 OUNCE

Nigger, you're the crazy one. People be wanting to kill you.
Are you talking about getting rid of your gun?

LITTLE JUAN

It's time, homey.

Kiss me, Little Juan.

MAX
(*suddenly out of character*)
Then he kisses her and we're out. OK.
(*pointing to the messenger*)
Is that for me?

The messenger gives Max the envelope. Max opens it.

INSERT LETTER:

Written neatly in blue crayon on paper torn from a spiral notebook. Dirk reads in Voice-over dripping with sarcasm.

Dear Max,
    I am sorry to say that I have secretly found out that Mr Blume is having an affair with Miss Cross. My first suspicions came when I saw them Frenching at the museum, and then I knew for sure when they went skinny dipping in Mr Blume's swimming pool, giving each other hand jobs while you were taking a nap on the front porch. Why am I telling you this now? Because you're such a *good friend*. Take care, pal.

Fondly,
Dirk Calloway

EXT. MISS CROSS'S HOUSE – NIGHT

Mr Blume puts on his jacket as he walks down the front path from Miss Cross's house. He gets in his Bentley and starts the engine. He looks in the rearview mirror and sees the glowing red tip of a cigarette. He wheels around fast.

Max is sitting in the backseat smoking a cigarette.

MR BLUME
Max!

MAX
How was she, Herman?

MR BLUME

Jesus Christ!

MAX

Was she good? I bet she was. Although I wouldn't know, cause I never screwed her.

Blume flicks on the lights. Max has tears all over his face.

(*with bitter contempt*)
Going skinny dipping while I took a nap. Are you comfortable, Max? I'll just be out back nude getting hand jobs with the woman you love.

MR BLUME
(*frowns*)
We never went skinny dipping.

MAX

Sure, you didn't. And next you're going to tell me you didn't just walk out of her house at two o'clock in the morning.

MR BLUME
(*pause*)
I'm in love with her.

MAX

Well, I was in love with her first. And all that crap about, I don't think she's that great, I don't think she's right for you, Max. That was all bullshit, wasn't it?

Silence.

Do you think she's in love with you?

MR BLUME

I don't know.

MAX

Well, I guarantee you she's not. And she never will be.

MR BLUME

Look, Max –

MAX

I saved Latin!

Max glares at Mr Blume. He shakes his head.

What'd *you* ever do?

INT. CLASSROOM – DAY

Miss Cross's class. A little boy named Benjamin reads his story in front of the class. Miss Cross sits in a chair at the back. Max appears in the doorway.

BENJAMIN

On the planet I'm from the sun only comes out once a year. That is –

Max coughs loudly. Miss Cross turns around. Max motions to her. She holds up her index finger for him to wait.

That is why my skin is the color of a cloud, said the old –

MAX
(*loudly*)

I just came by to thank you for wrecking my life.

Max slams the door.

EXT. QUADRANGLE – DAY

Max stands alone smoking a cigarette in front of a pile of leaves. A Lawn Crew is raking in the background.

Max strikes a match, throws it on the leaves, and watches sadly as the leaves burn and smoke rises black into the crisp autumn air. He takes off his Rushmore blazer and throws it on the fire. He looks up at the sky and says quietly:

MAX

Sic transit gloria, Mr Blume. *Sic transit gloria.*

EXT. PARK – DAY

A cold day. Dry leaves fall from the trees in the park.

Mrs Blume comes down the path to Max sitting alone on a bench. Max is dressed in blue jeans, a plaid shirt, a ski cap, and a huge down parka. Mrs Blume is wearing a topcoat and gloves. Max stands up to shake hands with her.

MAX

Thank you for meeting me.

MRS BLUME
(coldly)

You're welcome.

MAX

Would you like a sandwich?

Silence. Mrs Blume looks around the park.

MRS BLUME

All right.

She sits down. Max takes two sandwiches out of his backpack.

MAX

I have tuna fish and I have peanut butter and jelly. I'm sorry it's not something more exotic.

MRS BLUME

I'll take the tuna fish.

Max gives her the tuna fish sandwich.

75

MAX

Milk or apple juice?

Max holds out the two drinks. Mrs Blume just stares at him.

You want me to cut to the chase?

Silence. Max puts down his sandwich and gathers his thoughts.

OK. As you know, Mr Blume and I used to be friends.

MRS BLUME

I have no idea what the relationship is between you and
Herman. Honestly, I find it very bizarre.

MAX
(*taken aback*)

What do you mean to imply?

MRS BLUME

I'm not *implying* anything. You make a very strange couple.
It's too bad Herman doesn't have that kind of affection for his
own children.

MAX

Well, I'm sure he does.

MRS BLUME

No, he doesn't.

MAX

I know you don't really mean that.

MRS BLUME
(*angry*)

Of course, I do.

MAX

From his perspective it's –

MRS BLUME

Why did you call me?

MAX

That's what I'm trying to tell you.

MRS BLUME
(*icily*)

Please. Get to the point.

MAX

Gladly. Your husband's banging a school teacher, pardon my
French. I thought you should know.

Silence.

MRS BLUME

Why are you telling me this? Are you trying to hurt Mr
Blume? Or are you trying to hurt me?

MAX

I have no reason to want to hurt you.

MRS BLUME

Then you're trying to hurt Herman.

MAX

That's correct.

INT. THE BILBY-FLICKENGER HOTEL – NIGHT

*The vast lobby of the Bilby-Flickenger. Mr Blume is leaning against the
counter at the front desk. His luggage fills up two carts beside him. A
faint smile plays across his lips as he stares off into space. The Concierge
is checking him in.*

CONCIERGE

And how long will you be staying with us, Mr Blume?

MR BLUME

Indefinitely. I'm getting a divorce.

CONCIERGE
(*typing away*)

Very good, sir.

Mr Blume yells to the little Bellman.

MR BLUME

Yo!

*The Bellman looks up. Mr Blume waves. The Bellman waves back.
The Concierge gives Mr Blume his room key.*

> CONCIERGE
>
> Here you are, Mr Blume. Charles will show you to your
> room.

> MR BLUME
>
> Wonderful. Where's the pool, by the way? I might take a dip
> before dinner.

> CONCIERGE
>
> It's on the roof, sir.

> MR BLUME
>
> Terrific!

*Mr Blume gets on the elevator with the Bellman. The Bellman looks at
him and smiles.*

> BELLMAN
>
> You certainly seem happy today, sir.

> MR BLUME
>
> You bet your little ass I am, shorty. I lost my family. But I
> gained a woman I love.

> BELLMAN
>
> Not a bad trade-off.

INT. HOTEL ROOM – DAY

*The living room of Mr Blume's suite. Mr Blume is dressed in a bathrobe
with The Bilby-Flickenger stitched on the pocket. He sits at his table
having breakfast and reading the newspaper. There is a little basket in
front of him with a jar of honey in it. A note attached to the jar says,
'Enjoy your stay'.*

*A little bug flies around Mr Blume's head. He swats it away and keeps
reading.*

*Two more bugs come buzzing around him. Mr Blume looks up and
frowns. They're bees. Mr Blume slaps at his neck and jumps to his feet
as he gets stung.*

MR BLUME

Shit!

Bees are circling all over the room. Mr Blume looks around frantically. He sees something at the bottom of the front door. It is a little plastic tube with bees crawling out of it and taking off.

INT. BASEMENT – DAY

Max comes out of the freight elevator wearing a red room service jacket with The Bilby-Flickenger stitched on the pocket. He has a wooden box with Rushmore Beekeepers stencilled on it. Max throws the jacket in a laundry cart and goes out the back door.

EXT. GROVER CLEVELAND HIGH SCHOOL – DAY

Mr Blume gets out of his car in the driveway at Grover Cleveland. He opens the trunk and takes out a set of steel cable cutters. He goes over to the bike racks and cuts the lock off Max's ten-speed.

Mr Blume lays the bicycle on the ground in front of his car and runs over it. Then he throws the car in reverse and goes over it again. He picks up the destroyed bicycle and takes it back to the bike racks and wraps the lock back around it.

The small Indian groundskeeper we saw earlier on the roof is driving by in a Volkswagen Beetle. He frowns at Mr Blume. Mr Blume hurries back to his car.

79

EXT. BLUME INTERNATIONAL CONCRETE – DAY

*The front gates of the concrete plant. Max rides up on an old
grandmother's bicycle with fenders and a handlebar basket. He's got a
black duffel bag strapped to his back.*

Max waves to the Security Guard. The guard waves back:

> SECURITY GUARD
> Hey, Max!

*Max rides on to the lot and pulls over next to Mr Blume's Bentley. He
leans his bike against the car door. He unzips his duffel bag and slides
underneath the car.*

EXT. RUSHMORE – DAY

*Mr Blume pulls into the driveway to pick up the twins from school.
There is a lot of traffic and kids are running around everywhere. Mr
Blume taps the brakes. Nothing happens. He flies toward the back of a
parked station wagon.*

*He jerks the steering wheel and bounces up on to the sidewalk. The car
pops through a wooden fence and rolls across the grass into the
quadrangle.*

*The Indian Groundskeeper is raking leaves as the car goes past him. He
watches as it crunches over some bushes and scrapes against a stone
wall. It rolls to a stop in the middle of the quad.*

Mr Blume gets out of the car and looks at the damage. He looks over at the white-haired Indian Groundskeeper.

The Groundskeeper goes back to his raking.

EXT. PARKING LOT – DAY

Mr Blume stands beside a tow truck. He is giving a statement to a Police Officer.

> MR BLUME
> He's about five three, a hundred and twelve pounds, black hair, oval face, pale complexion.

INT. GROVER CLEVELAND HIGH SCHOOL – DAY

Kids watch from classrooms up and down the hall as Max is escorted away in handcuffs by the Police. Max has a hardened expression on his face.

INT. POLICE STATION – DAY

The county lock-up. Mr Fischer watches through bullet-proof glass as Max walks down a long, lonely corridor.

The door buzzes open. Max comes into the waiting room.

> MAX
> Thanks for bailing me out, Dad. Can you drop me off at

Rushmore? I got to go get a teacher fired.

> MR FISCHER
> (*hesitates*)
> You think that's wise, Max?

> MAX
> (*angry*)
> Dad. Please. Stay out of it.

EXT. RUSHMORE – DAY

Max walks into the quadrangle with a cold expression on his face. It is Hallow'een and there is a jack-o-lantern on the steps. Lots of kids are dressed in costumes.

Suddenly, Max is being pelted with rocks. He looks around frantically and sees Dirk and a long-haired kid named Tommy Stallings as they set upon him.

Dirk is dressed as a sorcerer. Tommy has on a karate outfit with a black belt. Max runs for cover behind some bushes.

> MAX
> What are you doing? Are you crazy?

> DIRK
> You're trespassing! This is private property!

More rocks sail past Max. A pine cone hits him in the head.

> MAX
> Wait a minute! Stop!

Max raises his hands in the air. Dirk motions for Tommy to hold his fire. Max slowly stands up.

> Let's have a truce for a second. I want to talk.

They meet out in the open. Tommy follows with a rock in each hand. Silence.

> What's this all about?

Dirk stares at Max for a long minute.

                              DIRK
Did you say my mother gave you a hand job?

                              MAX
                            (*shocked*)
What?

                              DIRK
                            (*steely*)
Did you say it.

                              MAX
Who told you that goddamn lie?

Silence.

Never mind. I know who said it. And I'm going to stick a
knife in his heart. And I'm going to send him back to Ireland
in a bodybag.

                             TOMMY
He's from Scotland.

                              MAX
Well, tell that stupid mick he just made my list of things to do
today. I'm going to pop a cap in his ass.

INT. TEAROOM – DAY

*A little salon with Persian rugs. There is a fire in the fireplace and a
harpsichord plays softly on the radio. Dr Guggenheim is sitting at a little
table having tea with Max.*

*Dr Guggenheim has several bottles of prescription medicine in front of
him and a blanket wrapped around him like a shawl. He stares at Max
stonily. There is a manila envelope on the table in between them.*

                              MAX
Did you receive the package?

Dr Guggenheim motions to the envelope. Max nods.

Good. I just wanted to inform you about what's going on.

Dr Guggenheim stares at Max with contempt.

DR GUGGENHEIM
I never took you for an informer, Max.

MAX
(*frowns*)
What's that supposed to mean?

Silence. Max reaches out to take the envelope. Dr Guggenheim slams his hand on it and leans across the table at Max.

DR GUGGENHEIM
(*fiercely*)
She resigned this morning. Before I even got your little snapshots. So your latest attempt at sabotage has backfired.

MAX
(*pause*)
But she's one of the best teachers you've got.
(*yelling*)
How could you let her resign?

DR GUGGENHEIM
(*yelling back at him*)
Why are you trying to get her fired?

MAX
You stupid old fool! I'm trying to win her back!

Dr Guggenheim starts coughing and turning red. He knocks the envelope off the table and the pictures spill out all over the floor.

INSERT PHOTOGRAPHS ON THE FLOOR:

They're of Mr Blume and Miss Cross kissing in the window of a Chinese restaurant.

INT. MISS CROSS'S CLASSROOM – DAY

A crew of Movers are rolling one of Miss Cross' aquariums out of the room on a dolly as Max comes to the door. Miss Cross is on the other side of the classroom taking down a map from the wall. Her books and papers are stacked in boxes.

Max watches her in silence for a minute before saying:

84

                            MAX

   Miss Cross?

She turns around to look at Max. Silence.

                         MISS CROSS

   Hi, Max.

                            MAX

   You need any help?

                         MISS CROSS

   No. I have it.

She pricks her finger and holds it to her mouth.

   Dammit.

Max starts to go in the room to help her.

                            MAX

   Here. Let me see.

                         MISS CROSS

   No. Please, don't come in here. Look. I'm sorry I hurt you.
   I'm sorry I love your friend instead of you. But just. Please,
   Max.

Miss Cross has tears in her eyes. Max goes slowly toward her.

                            MAX

   You honestly believe that you love Blume instead of me?

                         MISS CROSS

   Yes.

                            MAX

   You'll forgive me if I won't take your word for that.

                         MISS CROSS

   Stop. If you don't stop with that ping-pong talk, I'm going to
   lose it. Do you understand me?

Max takes Miss Cross's hand and kisses it. She pulls her hand away.
Max tries to embrace her. They struggle and Miss Cross overpowers
Max. She holds his arms behind his back.

                            85

Let me go!

Max struggles some more. Miss Cross pushes him hard across the room. Max smashes into some chairs and knocks over a desk. He yells at her:

I got kicked out because of you!

MISS CROSS
You got kicked out because –

MAX
Rushmore was my life. Now you are!

MISS CROSS
No, I'm not!

Silence.

What do you really think is going to happen between us? You think we're going to have sex?

Max looks shocked.

MAX
That's kind of a cheap way to put it, isn't it?

MISS CROSS
(*pause*)
Not if you've ever fucked before, it isn't.

MAX
(*stunned*)
Oh, my God.

MISS CROSS
How would you put it to your friends? Do you want to finger me? Or maybe I could give you a hand job in the back of a Jaguar. Would that put an end to all of this?

Miss Cross moves toward Max with her hand outstretched. Max retreats backwards, banging into the desks and chairs. Miss Cross stops.

Please. Get out of my classroom.

Max walks out of the room and stands in the doorway.

Miss Cross turns away and goes back to taking down her maps from the wall. Max watches her for a minute.

Max leaves.

EXT. QUADRANGLE – DAY

Max comes out the door of the lower school in a daze. Magnus Buchan is sitting on a bench eating some candy. He is wearing the uniform of a Green Beret. He sees Max and laughs.

> MAGNUS
> Fischer, ya spotty fucker!

> MAX
> Hello, Magnus.

> MAGNUS
> Got any hand jobs lately?

> MAX
> No, I haven't.

Dirk appears with some of his friends.

> MAGNUS
> Hey, Dirk! Look who's here. Your stepfather! Waitin' for your mum so he can get a piece.

Dirk is very embarrassed. He frowns and looks at the ground. Max stares at Magnus with bitter contempt.

> MAX
> Your mind is as warped as your ear, Buchan.

> MAGNUS
> *(standing up)*
> Don't get nasty, brother.

Max breaks into a sprint straight at Magnus.

Magnus draws back and nails Max in the cheek. Max goes down but gets right back up. They throw a flurry of punches at each other's faces. Some kids come running over to watch.

Max tackles Magnus around the legs. Magnus throws a hard punch

87

straight down at the top of Max's head. Max goes limp and collapses to the ground.

CUT TO:

Max's eyes opening. He is lying on his back in a pile of leaves. A bunch of little kids have circled around him.

Max's nose bleeds profusely. One of his eyes is swollen shut. He has little cuts all over his face. His shirt is torn more or less in half. He looks up at Dirk standing over him. He lifts up his hand to Dirk.

MAX
We got him, Dirk. We got him.

But Dirk does not take Max's hand. He turns away.

EXT. CEMETERY – DAY

Mr Blume spots Max sitting Indian-style at the foot of his mother's grave on a cold, grey day. The simple epitaph reads 'Eloise Fischer, beloved wife of Bert and mother of Max.' Written below it says: 'the paths of glory lead but to the grave'. Mr Blume approaches warily.

MR BLUME
Max?

Max looks up. There is a quiet sadness about him and his voice has lost all feeling of possibility.

MAX
Hi, Mr Blume.

Mr Blume stands there in silence.

MR BLUME
You wanted to meet?

MAX
When?

MR BLUME
Right now. You said you wanted to put an end to this nonsense.

MAX

Oh. Yeah. I was going to try to have that oak tree fall on you.

Max jerks his thumb over his shoulder. Mr Blume looks at a massive oak tree hanging precariously by the roots.

MR BLUME

That big one? That would have really pancaked me.
(*pause*)
What stopped you?

MAX
(*shrugs*)
What's the point? She loves you.

Max gets up. They look at each other in silence.

So long, Mr Blume.

Max starts to walk away. Mr Blume calls after him:

MR BLUME

She's my Rushmore, Max.

MAX
(*without stopping*)
Yeah, I know. She was mine, too.

Max leaves the cemetery. Mr Blume stands alone. He goes over to the tree and taps it. It comes crashing down.

November

THANKSGIVING MONTAGE:

Max walks down the street with his lunch in a brown paper bag. He goes into the barber's shop. He nods hello to his father and puts on a white barber's jacket. He has a blank, hollow expression on his face.

Max gives an old man a haircut while the old man reads the paper. Max gives another old man a shave. Max combs another old man's hair and holds up a mirror so he can see the back.

Dirk rides past the barber's shop on his little French three-speed. He circles back and looks at Max taking the trash out to the dumpster. Max doesn't see him. Dirk pedals away.

Margaret knocks on the front door of the Fischers' house. Mr Fischer opens the door. He and Margaret talk for a minute. Mr Fischer shakes his head sadly. Margaret nods.

Mr Fischer closes the door as Margaret walks out to the sidewalk. She looks back at the house. Max is sitting in the window, staring off into space. Margaret hesitates. She goes across the yard to the window.

She taps on the glass. Max looks out at her. She waves to him. Max closes the curtains.

Margaret turns away sadly and walks off down the sidewalk.

*Max and Mr Fischer sit in front of the TV having TV Thanksgiving
dinners as they watch a football game. Mr Fischer looks at Max. Max
stares at the television set.*

TITLE:

December

INT. BARBER'S SHOP – EVENING

*There is a wreath on the door and some blinking lights are strung up.
The last customer of the day comes out and walks away through the
snow. Mr Fischer is putting on his sweater while Max washes some
combs and scissors in the sink.*

MR FISCHER
It's been nice having your company here at the shop, Max.

Max nods.

Have you put any more thought into giving school another
shot?

*Max shakes his head. Mr Fischer puts on a hunting cap with earflaps
and a down parka. He zips it up. Pause.*

Max. I like being a barber. I'm good at it and I enjoy it. But I
always thought you'd try a different line of work.

MAX
Like what?

MR FISCHER
I don't know. You talked about being a diplomat. Or a
senator.

MAX
Pipe dreams, Dad. Nothing but pipe dreams. I'm a barber's
son.

*Max turns on the radio and goes back to washing the combs and
scissors. Mr Fischer sighs. He puts on his gloves. He goes out the door.*

Max flips the sign on the door from open to closed. He takes off his barber's jacket and hangs it on the coatrack. He goes into the back room.

He comes back into the shop carrying a broom. He stops.

Dirk is sitting in one of the barber's chairs across the room. Silence. Max starts sweeping the floor.

> *(not looking at him)*
Hello, Dirk.

DIRK
Hi, Max.

MAX
What can I do for you?

DIRK
I thought I might get a haircut.

MAX
We're closed.

Dirk nods. Max keeps sweeping.

DIRK
Well. I just wanted to tell you I'm sorry I threw rocks at you that day.
> *(getting up)*
But I guess I'll go now.

Dirk sets a little gift-wrapped present on the counter.

Merry Christmas

Max stops sweeping and looks over at Dirk.

MAX
What in the hell is that?

Dirk shrugs. Max goes over to the counter and picks up the present. He unwraps it. It is a Swiss Army Knife with an inscription on it.

INSERT SWISS ARMY KNIFE:

Max Fischer
Rushmore Yankee
1985–1997

Max looks at the knife for a minute. He says wearily:

OK. Sit down.

Dirk sits back down in the barber's chair. Max puts his white jacket back on and starts giving Dirk a haircut. There is just the sound of scissors snipping for a minute.

DIRK
Have you heard the news?

MAX
I doubt it. I don't really follow the news any more.

DIRK
Dr Guggenheim had a stroke.

MAX
I'll send him a box of candy.

DIRK
Maybe you ought to go visit him.

Max stops snipping. Pause.

MAX
No, thanks.

Max starts snipping again.

EXT. BARBER'S SHOP – EVENING

Dirk comes out of the barber's shop with a terrible haircut. He waves to Max and rides off on his three-speed.

INT. BARBER'S SHOP – EVENING

Max waves back to Dirk. He reaches into the cooler and takes out a bottle of Schlitz. He pops it open with the bottle opener on the Swiss Army knife. He drinks a sip and looks out into the lightly falling snow. He says quietly to himself:

MAX

I always thought *I'd* be the one to give him a stroke.

INT. HOSPITAL ROOM — NIGHT

Dr Guggenheim is in his hospital bed with his eyes half shut and a bunch of plastic tubes sticking out of him. Mrs Guggenheim sits in a chair at the foot of the bed reading a biography of Churchill. She looks exhausted.

Max appears in the open doorway. He has a bouquet of violets in his hand. He knocks.

MAX

Mrs Guggenheim?

Mrs Guggenheim looks up. Her face brightens and she goes to greet Max.

MRS GUGGENHEIM

Hello, Max. How are you?

MAX
(*desolately*)

Fine, thanks.

Max starts to shake hands, but Mrs Guggenheim hugs him and kisses him on the cheek instead. Max is caught a little off guard by this. There is lipstick on his cheek.

MRS GUGGENHEIM

These are glorious. Let me put them in some water. Sit down.

She takes the flowers and points to a chair beside the bed. Max sits down and stares at Dr Guggenheim while Mrs Guggenheim puts the violets in a vase.

MAX

Should I say hello to Dr Guggenheim? Or can he not hear anything?

MRS GUGGENHEIM

Oh, no. He can hear you.

                              MAX
OK.
                            (*sadly*)
Hello, old timer. It's Max Fischer. I was just thinking about
you the other day. And Rushmore. And I –

*Dr Guggenheim's eyes suddenly open. Max is taken aback. Dr
Guggenheim looks at Max suspiciously and whispers:*

                      DR GUGGENHEIM
What do you want?

Mrs Guggenheim looks up quickly. Max hesitates.

                              MAX
I just came by to pay my respects.

                      DR GUGGENHEIM
                            (*frowns*)
No, you didn't. You don't respect anybody.

*Dr Guggenheim tries to spit at Max, but his mouth is too dry. Mrs
Guggenheim comes over to them.*

                     MRS GUGGENHEIM
Nelson?

Dr Guggenheim mutters deliriously:

                      DR GUGGENHEIM
Dammit. Goddammit.

*Mrs Guggenheim takes Dr Guggenheim's hand and holds it. He calms
down. His eyes close and he relaxes. Silence.*

Mrs Guggenheim looks to Max.

                     MRS GUGGENHEIM
That's the first thing he's said in ten days.

Max nods. He sits quietly beside the bed.

                              MAX
You think he recognized me?

                    MRS GUGGENHEIM
    No, honey. He's just delir –

                    DR GUGGENHEIM
                       (*groaning*)
    It's Fischer.

    CUT TO:

*Dirk hidden in the bushes across the street from the hospital. He checks
his watch. He raises his binoculars to his eyes and looks on mysteriously
as:*

Mr Blume pulls into the parking lot in his Bentley.

Dirk makes a quick notation in his spiral with a blue crayon.

    INSERT NOTEBOOK:

         5:25 Fischer arrives via old woman's bicycle
         5:47 Blume arrives via black Bentley.

INT. ELEVATOR – NIGHT

*Max rides down in the elevator with a Nurse and a wheezing Old
Woman in a wheelchair. The doors open in the lobby and Max waits
while the nurse wheels out the old woman.*

*Then he sees Mr Blume in front of him, waiting for the elevator. He has
a bouquet of carnations in one hand and a diet Coke in the other. He
has a black eye under his sunglasses. He is very disheveled.*

                    MR BLUME
    Hey, amigo.

                      MAX
    You look horrible.

                    MR BLUME
    You don't look too great yourself. Good to see you.

                      MAX
    You here to see Guggenheim?

                    MR BLUME
    Yeah. Your partner told me he was under the weather.

                       96

                               MAX
                            (*frowns*)
What partner?

Silence. Mr Blume shrugs.

                            MR BLUME
OK. If you want to play it that way. You getting off?

                               MAX
I'll ride up with you.

                            MR BLUME
                          (*getting on*)
Suit yourself.

*Mr Blume presses the button for the fourteenth floor. The doors close and
they go up. Mr Blume takes out a little airline bottle of vodka and pours
some into his Diet Coke. He swirls it around and drinks a sip.*

                               MAX
Who gave you the shiner?

                            MR BLUME
Honestly? I don't actually know. It was either Ronny or
Donny. But I can't tell the difference anymore.

                               MAX
Well, he really clocked you.

                            MR BLUME
Yeah? Well. Kids don't like their parents to get divorced.

                               MAX
I don't blame them.

                            MR BLUME
Me, neither.

Silence.

                               MAX
How is she?

                            MR BLUME
I wouldn't know.

                               97

MAX

Why not?

MR BLUME

Because I haven't seen her in six weeks.

MAX
(*frowns*)

What happened?

Mr Blume shrugs.

MAX

She left you?

Mr Blume nods.

How come? I thought she loved you.

MR BLUME

So did I. I guess maybe I am too old for her, after all.

MAX
(*sadly*)

Maybe so. Maybe so.

MR BLUME

She's still in love with the dead guy, anyway.

MAX

You mean Edward Appleby?

MR BLUME

Oh, yeah. She's fucked up.

Mr Blume lights a new cigarette. Max points to Mr Blume's first cigarette, balanced on the handrail.

MAX

You've already got one going, Mr Blume.

Mr Blume picks up his first cigarette and puts it in the opposite corner of his mouth from the second. He smiles at Max through the smoke. They get to the fourteenth floor and the doors open.

MR BLUME

Adios, amigo.

Max waves goodbye. But Mr Blume does not get off the elevator. He bends over and puts his hands on his knees and takes a series of deep breaths. The doors start to close. He reaches out and holds them open. Max looks concerned.

MAX

Are you OK?

Mr Blume looks up at Max. He laughs and shakes his head.

MR BLUME

I'm kind of lonely these days.

Mr Blume sighs. He gets off the elevator. The doors close behind him as Max watches him walk down the hall.

CUT TO:

Dirk's binoculars:

Max comes out of the hospital and stands quietly in the cold for a minute. He gets on his mother's old bicycle. He rides off down the street.

EXT. THE FISCHERS' HOUSE – DAY

Max opens the Fischers' garage door. His smashed-up ten-speed hangs from a peg on the wall. He takes it down and carries it out of the garage.

INT. MISS CROSS'S HOUSE – NIGHT

Miss Cross is sitting up in her bed reading Treasure Island *and listening to the radio. She is wearing pale blue pajamas. There is a knock on her windowpane. She looks up.*

She hears someone trying to open the window. She gets up and pulls open the blinds. Max is outside on the roof wearing his parka and ski cap in the falling snow. He waves.

MISS CROSS

Max!

Miss Cross opens the window.

99

What are you doing here?

> MAX
> (*dazed*)

I don't know. Jesus. They came at me out of nowhere. It was –

> MISS CROSS

What?

> MAX

So sudden. I just –

> (*pause*)

I'm sorry. Can I use your phone? I just got hit by a car.

Max points down at his destroyed ten-speed in the street under a street lamp. Parts are scattered all around it.

> MISS CROSS

Oh, my God. Are you OK?

> MAX
> (*disoriented*)

Hm? What'd you say?

Miss Cross notices a little cut over Max's eye. She lifts up the front of Max's ski cap. There is blood all over his forehead. She looks shocked.

> MISS CROSS

Come inside.

> MAX
> (*climbing in*)

Thank you.

Max goes to Miss Cross's bed. He lies down and stares at the ceiling.

Miss Cross goes into the bathroom. She puts on a white bathrobe and gets some cotton balls and hydrogen peroxide out of the medicine cabinet.

Max looks around the room.

So this is where it all happens.

MISS CROSS
(*from the bathroom*)

All what happens?

MAX

I wouldn't know.

Miss Cross comes back into the bedroom.

Why'd you dump Blume?

Miss Cross stops. Pause.

MISS CROSS

That's none of your business.

MAX

I know it's not. But I just got hit by a car. And I'm a little
confused right now. I mean, I thought you dumped me for
Blume. Then I hear –

MISS CROSS

I never dumped you. Because we were never going out.

MAX
(*snaps*)

Don't play semantics with me.

Miss Cross frowns. Max says quietly:

Excuse me. I don't mean to snap at you. It would just help
me if you would talk to me for a minute. And tell me what
happened.

Silence. Miss Cross sighs.

MISS CROSS

OK. A. He's married. B. He hates himself. And C. I mean, he
smashed your bicycle, didn't he?

MAX
(*pause*)

My previous bicycle, yes.

MISS CROSS

Well, what kind of person does something like that?

MAX

I don't know.

(*pause*)

War does funny things to men.

Silence. Miss Cross sits down in a rocking chair beside the bed. She opens the bottle of hydrogen peroxide.

He thinks you dumped him because of Edward Appleby.

MISS CROSS

What does that mean?

MAX

Well. I mean, you live in his room.

Max looks around the room. There are trophies and ribbons, a chemistry set, a poster from the Olympics, three large fish tanks, a picture of Jacques Cousteau, and some model planes in dogfights hanging from the ceiling.

With all his stuff. It's kind of –

MISS CROSS

I was married to him.

MAX
(*pause*)

I know you were.

Silence.

MISS CROSS

Although I will say Edward had more spark and character and imagination in one fingernail than Herman Blume has in his entire body.

MAX

One dead fingernail.

Miss Cross fixes Max with a hard stare.

MISS CROSS

Right. One dead fingernail.

Silence.

102

                    MAX
How'd he die, by the way?

                  MISS CROSS
He drowned.
                    (*pause*)
How'd your mother die?

                    MAX
She got cancer.

Miss Cross nods. She sighs.

                  MISS CROSS
Lie still for a minute. OK?

                    MAX
OK.

*Miss Cross pushes Max's hair back with her hand. She looks at him for
a minute. She touches the blood on his forehead with a cotton ball. She
stops.*

                  MISS CROSS
Is this fake blood?

                    MAX
                    (*pause*)
Yes, it is.

You know, you and Herman deserve each other. You're little children. Let me show you the door.

MAX

I'll just go back out the window.

Max gets up and goes over to the window. He climbs out on to the roof. He looks back to Miss Cross. Silence.

Goodbye, Miss Cross.

MISS CROSS

Goodbye, Max.

Max disappears into the darkness.

EXT. FIELD – DAY

Max and Dirk are in the middle of a field on a freezing cold afternoon. Dirk is flying a kite. It is blue with a red tail. Dirk stomps his feet, and even with his mittens on he has to blow into his hands to keep warm.

Max sits on the ground smoking a cigarette and drinking a can of Schlitz wrapped in a paper bag. He is wearing blue jeans and a thin undershirt with a pack of cigarettes rolled into one of the sleeves. He is shivering in the cold.

MAX

People hate me.

DIRK

That's not true.

MAX

Guggenheim tried to spit on me. Poor old guy couldn't even spit. And Blume and Cross:
    (*shakes his head*)
They can't stand me. I ruined their whole relationship.

Dirk looks down at Max's hands, which are turning blue.

DIRK

You should put your mittens on.

MAX
Oh. They're already numb.

Tears start streaming down Max's face. Dirk looks worried.

I'm sorry about what I said about your mother giving me a hand job.

DIRK

I know, Max. Listen. I'm sorry I didn't take your hand when Buchan kicked your ass.

MAX
(shrugs)

I got a few licks in.

DIRK

You should put on a sweater.

MAX

I'm awfully comfortable.

Silence. Dirk looks up curiously.

DIRK

What's that?

There is a faint buzzing noise off in the distance. It begins to grow louder. Max frowns.

MAX

I don't know. But it's –

A model fighter plane suddenly shoots out over the trees. It is a World War II Spitfire. It circles around Dirk's kite and executes a rapid series of rolls and dives.

Max and Dirk notice the Pilot standing a few yards away from them working the remote controls. The Pilot is a girl in grey tights and a short camel-hair coat. She has a scarf over the lower half of her face.

She lands the plane in the short grass. She looks to Max and Dirk. Silence.

Nice landing.

The Pilot holds out a little piece of paper torn from a spiral notebook.

PILOT

Is this your handwriting?

Max stands up and takes the piece of paper. There is a note written on it in blue crayon.

INSERT PIECE OF PAPER:

Please come to the field near the pond at
3.30 PM this afternoon. Thank you very much.

Max looks to Dirk. Dirk is staring up at his kite.

MAX

No. But it looks familiar.

Max gives the piece of paper back to the girl. She lowers her scarf and we see that she is Margaret Yang.

Do you know Dirk Calloway?

MARGARET

I don't think so.

MAX

Dirk, this is Margaret Yang.

Dirk nods. Margaret waves to him.

I heard about your science fair project on Action 13 the other day. They said the Navy was going to buy it from you.

Margaret is polite but cold.

MARGARET

Not anymore.

MAX

Why not?

MARGARET

Because it was a fake.

MAX

What do you mean?

MARGARET
(*sighs*)

I faked all the results.

MAX

Why?

MARGARET

Because it didn't work. I thought it would, but it didn't.

MAX
(*in disbelief*)

You mean it was all bullshit?

MARGARET

Not all of it. Just the parts I didn't get right.

Max stares at her. He says quietly:

MAX

That's exactly the way I would've handled that situation.

MARGARET

Well. It's nothing to be proud of.

MAX

But it's true.

Max looks hypnotized.

MARGARET

You were a real jerk to me.

MAX
(*pause*)
I know. I'm sorry, Margaret.

Silence.

MARGARET

Well. Anyway. Nice to see you.

Max nods.

Margaret presses a button on her remote control box. The plane begins to roll along the field. Margaret steers as it takes off and climbs quickly. Max and Dirk watch the plane circle away over the trees.

The fuselage suddenly bursts into flames and the plane goes into a dive with black smoke streaming out of its tail. It disappears among the trees in the distance.

Margaret looks shocked. She runs off after her plane.

Silence. Max looks to Dirk.

MAX

You set me up.

Dirk does not respond. Max says wistfully:

Not bad, not bad. The child has become the father of the man.

Max sighs. Dirk says quietly:

DIRK

You want me to take over for a while?

Max looks to Dirk. Dirk smiles sadly. He hands the kite over to Max and they both watch it flying against the gray clouds. Something begins to change in Max's face. His eyes narrow. He whispers to himself in a steely voice:

MAX

I wonder what would happen if I did a little something like this:

Max jerks the kite string back and forth with a dramatic sweeping motion. The kite dips and makes a quick, graceful pirouette.

Max looks to Dirk. Dirk is impressed. Max looks back up to the kite.

Take dictation please.

Dirk hesitates. He quickly pulls a little notebook out of his pocket.

Possible candidates for Kite Flying Society.

Dirk smiles and starts writing.

Duncan Wright. David Connors. Murray Marshall. Margaret Yang. Ronny and Donny Blume. Magnus Buchan.

The list continues as we:

DISSOLVE TO:

EXT. BARBER'S SHOP – DAY

Mr Blume stands on the sidewalk in front of the barber's shop. He stares off into the distance. He has his hands in his pockets and his hair is blowing in the wind.

Mr Fischer is inside reading the sports page.

A cab pulls up and splashes water on Mr Blume, but he does not appear to notice. Max gets out of the cab. He is dressed in a beautiful green velvet suit and a bow tie. He smiles.

MAX

Thanks for meeting me, Mr Blume.

MR BLUME

What can I do for you?

Max hands Mr Blume a little white cardboard box. Mr Blume frowns.

What's this?

Max shrugs. Mr Blume starts to open the box. Max flinches away like the box is going to explode. Mr Blume stops. Max smiles and motions for Mr Blume to go ahead. Mr Blume opens the box. There are two

little pins inside. They are both slightly charred around the edges.

> MAX
>
> That's the Perfect Attendance Award and the Punctuality Award. I got those at Rushmore. I thought you could choose which one you like more, and you could wear that one and I could wear the other.

Mr Blume's face softens. He nods slowly. He studies the pins and says quietly:

> MR BLUME
>
> I'll take Punctuality.

> MAX
>
> OK.

They put the pins in their lapels.

> MR BLUME
>
> Thank you.

Max nods. He smiles.

> MAX
>
> Come on. Let's go inside.

Max motions to the barber's shop. Mr Blume looks confused.

INT. BARBER'S SHOP – DAY

Mr Blume follows Max into the barber's shop. Mr Fischer looks up from his newspaper:

> MR FISCHER
> Well, look what the cat dragged in.

> MAX
> Sorry I'm late. I want you to meet somebody.
> *(looks to Mr Blume)*
> Mr Blume, this is my father, Bert Fischer.

Silence. Mr Blume nods slowly.

> MR BLUME
> Nice to meet you, Mr Fischer.

> MR FISCHER
> *(smiles)*
> Mr Fischer's my father's name. Call me Bert.

> MR BLUME
> *(pause)*

OK, Bert.

> MR FISCHER
> Max tells me you could use a haircut.

Mr Blume hesitates.

Let's have a look at you.

Mr Blume sits down in one of the barber's chairs and looks in the mirror. Max and Mr Fischer stand on either side of him. Mr Blume looks terrible. He sighs deeply.

> MR BLUME
> I don't know, Bert.

> MR FISCHER
> Don't worry. It's a relatively painless procedure. We might have to throw in a shave, too. Max? Why don't you get Mr Blume a cup of coffee?

Max and Mr Blume come out of the barber's shop and walk quickly down the sidewalk. Mr Blume's hair is crisply cut and neatly combed, but his clothes still look very disheveled.

> MAX
>
> How much are you worth, by the way?

> MR BLUME
>
> I don't know.

> MAX
>
> Over ten million?

> MR BLUME
>
> Yeah. I guess so.

> MAX
>
> Good, good.

> MR BLUME
>
> Why?

> MAX
>
> Cause we're going to need all of it.

DECEMBER MONTAGE:

Christmas decorations are in evidence throughout the following scenes.

Max and Mr Blume watch a Jacques Cousteau film on 16mm in Mr Blume's office. Ernie runs the projector.

Max and Mr Blume visit a marine research facility. Mr Blume holds up a fish at the edge of a pool. A killer whale jumps out of the water and takes it in its teeth.

Max and Mr Blume sprint down the street and through the park in warm-up suits. They hurdle bushes and dodge traffic. They run into an empty football stadium and race up the bleachers.

Max's young architect shows Max and Mr Blume a miniature baseball diamond. The architect slides over the diamond an inch and puts a model of a building labeled The Cousteau–Blume Marine Observatory in its place.

A dozen Rushmore and Grover Cleveland Students are flying kites in a field. Max runs in front of them with his kite trailing behind him. The kite sails up into the air.

EXT. VACANT LOT – DAY

A large crowd of Rushmore students, parents and faculty has gathered around the vacant lot beside the baseball field. A huge banner says 'The Cousteau–Blume Marine Observatory'. There is a bulldozer and a cement truck at the back of the lot.

Max and Mr Blume shake hands for the yearbook photographer. Mr Blume is holding a gold shovel with a ribbon around it.

> MR BLUME
> She's not coming, is she?

> MAX
> (*pause*)
> It doesn't look good.

> MR BLUME
> Ah, shit, man. What the hell am I doing here?

Mr Blume throws down his shovel and starts to walk off. Max yells at him:

> MAX
> Dammit! How the hell did you ever get so rich? You're a quitter!

Mr Blume looks back at Max in shock.

> MR BLUME
> This cost me eight million dollars!

> MAX
> (*hesitates*)
> And that's all you're prepared to spend?

Silence.

EXT. THE FISCHERS' HOUSE – DAY

Max carries an old leather typewriter case into the backyard. He sets it down on a picnic table. The case has an inscription on it in gold letters.

INSERT TYPEWRITER CASE:

Bravo, Max! Love, Mom.

Max unzips the case. There is an old portable manual typewriter inside. Max rolls a piece of paper into it and starts typing furiously. He pauses to drink a sip of hot chocolate. He starts typing again.

TITLE:

January

EXT. WEBSTER SMALLEY SCHOOL FOR GIRLS – DAY

Webster Smalley is Rushmore's sister school. The doors to the lower school burst open and twenty-five first-grade girls in plaid jumpers run yelling on to the playground.

Miss Cross comes out of the building after the girls. She sees Max coming down the hill in his green suit.

MISS CROSS

I like your new suit.

MAX

Thanks.

MISS CROSS

Is that velvet?

Max nods. Miss Cross feels his lapel. It has his Perfect Attendance Award pin in it.

MAX

Sorry you couldn't make it to our little groundbreaking the other day. It's kind of a shame, since he's building it for you.

MISS CROSS

Well, you know, I never asked anybody to build me an aquarium. I'm not sure how that rumor got started.

MAX

Hm. Me, neither. You think Edward Appleby would've built you one?

Miss Cross thinks for a minute. She sounds surprised at her own response:

> MISS CROSS
>
> Yeah. He probably would've. If he had the money.

> MAX
> *(smiles)*
>
> That's what I thought. Blume's got a little more spark and vitality than you expected, hasn't he?

> MISS CROSS
>
> But the aquarium was *your* idea.

Max smiles and shrugs his shoulders.

> MAX
>
> Well, I gave it to my friend.

Max turns and starts walking away. He looks back over his shoulder and says:

> By the way, I still haven't fucked anybody yet. But I guess that's just the way it goes.

Miss Cross smiles sadly.

INSERT TEACHERS' MAILBOXES:

A cabinet of little slots where teachers get their mail and memos. Someone puts a little envelope into the slot marked Rosemary Cross.

INT. WAREHOUSE – DAY

Max stands at the counter in a huge construction supply warehouse. A Salesman says:

> SALESMAN
>
> Fifteen sticks?

> MAX
>
> Yes, please. And make the order out to Ready Demolition, Tucson, Arizona.

Max holds up a driver's license. The salesman looks at it and writes something on a clipboard. Max walks out of the warehouse with several large boxes over his shoulder. The boxes say DYNAMITE *on them in large red letters.*

EXT. STREET – DAY

Dirk comes out of a hiding place in the bushes as Max walks over with the dynamite. Dirk is holding a pellet gun.

> MAX
>
> Make sure these don't get wet.

Max hands Dirk the boxes and takes the pellet gun.

> I'll see you at three-fifteen.

Max starts walking away down the sidewalk.

> DIRK
>
> Where you going?

> MAX
> (*without stopping*)
>
> Rushmore. I got one last piece of unfinished business I got to attend to.

EXT. RUSHMORE – DAY

Max pumps his pellet gun about twenty times. He raises the stock to his shoulder as Magnus Buchan walks on to the quadrangle. He draws a bead on him and follows him in his sights as he passes by. He fires.

Magnus screams and grabs his only good ear. He spins around and sees Max cocking his pellet gun.

> MAGNUS

Fischer! Ya fuck!

> MAX

Hello, Magnus. I'd have shot you in the other ear, but it got blown off a long time ago.

Magnus starts to come at Max. Max points his weapon at him.

Not so fast.

Magnus stops.

I owed you that one. Now we're even.

> MAGNUS
> (*smiles crookedly*)

Not for long, kemosabe.

> MAX
> (*shrugs*)

We'll see.

Silence. Max hold Magnus at gunpoint.

I got a proposition for you.

> MAGNUS

Shove it up your mother's arse, ya little prick.

> MAX

I got to hand it to you, Magnus. You've got a way with words. You want to be in a play?

> MAGNUS
> (*puzzled*)

Don't piss with me, Fischer.

> MAX

I'm not pissing with you.
> (*reaching in his backpack*)

I brought you a script.

117

Max hands Magnus a script with a red cover.

MAGNUS

What's all this shite?

MAX

Nothing. I just think you're right for the part.

Magnus stares at Max. He says quietly:

MAGNUS

I always wanted to be in one of those frickin' plays of yours.

MAX

I know you did, mate.

Magnus looks at the script.

INSERT COVER OF PLAY:

HEAVEN AND HELL
a new play by Max Fischer
revised draft
Dramatists Guild registered

INT. GROVER CLEVELAND HIGH SCHOOL – NIGHT

The school auditorium.

We see many familiar faces in the audience: Mr Fischer, Dr Guggenheim in his wheelchair, Mrs Guggenheim, Mrs Calloway, Mrs Whitney, the Indian Groundskeeper, the yearbook photographer, Coach Beck, Ernie, Mr Holstead, Mr Adams, the Police who arrested Max, some Old Men from the barber's shop.

Miss Cross's friend John, whom Max humiliated at dinner after the Serpico play, is seated in the third row. He is dressed in a coat and tie.

An Usher directs Miss Cross to her seat. She is surprised to see that it is right next to Mr Blume's. She reluctantly sits down beside him. Mr Blume sees her.

MISS CROSS

Hi, Herman.

Mr Blume nods. He pulls his ticket out of his inside pocket and checks the seat number. He looks to Miss Cross. Miss Cross smiles.

Looks like Max pulled a fast one on us.

Mr Blume nods.

How's your aquarium coming along?

MR BLUME
Not too bad. It should be finished in October.

Miss Cross nods.

I just made a deal with a guy in Singapore for half a dozen electric eels.

MISS CROSS
That sounds good.

The lights go down. A spotlight appears and Max walks onstage in his green velvet suit. He goes to a microphone in the middle of the stage.

MAX
I don't usually do this, but this play means a lot to me, and I wanted to make a dedication. So I'll just say that this play is dedicated to the memory of my mother, Eloise Fischer. And to Edward Appleby. A friend of a friend.

Neither Mr Fischer nor Miss Cross were expecting this announcement, and they are moved by it.

MAX

Also you'll find a pair of safety glasses and some earplugs underneath your seats. Please feel free to use them. Thank you very much.

Max exits the stage and the audience applauds. There is a moment of rustling and whispering in the dark theater.

Then the curtain opens on:

Vietnam. Napalm smolders in the sky above the jungle.

Dirk runs onstage dressed in a Green Beret uniform and sunglasses. He has an M-16. He yells to Max as Max shimmies down out of a palm tree:

DIRK

Let's rock, Esposito!

MAX

Lock and load, Surf Boy!

There is an explosion and Max and Dirk run through the smoke. Suddenly the stage is swarmed by VC regulars. Everyone starts shooting at once.

Bursts of gunfire light up the audience's faces and smoke floats over their heads as we hear the sounds of jets flying over, bombs exploding, choppers taking off, and a soldier's voice screaming into his radio:

SOLDIER

Mayday! Mayday! Seven niner Almighty! Adjust your
coordinates!

*Some members of the audience put on their safety glasses and earplugs.
Woody stands nervously in the wings with a fire extinguisher.*

*One of the extras accidentally clubs Max in the temple with the butt of
his rifle. Max's eyes close. He crumples to the floor. The fighting stops.
The audience begins to murmur.*

Max opens his eyes. He sees the frightened soldiers looking down at him.

He grabs his M-16 and opens fire. The battle resumes.

INSERT SIGN WRITTEN IN CALLIGRAPHY:

Intermission.

*The sign is leaning on an easel in front of the curtain. Little roses and
tulips are painted around its edges.*

INT. DRESSING ROOM – NIGHT

*Actors run around frantically backstage. Max has a Band-Aid on his
forehead. He is touching up a gory make-up effect over Dirk's eye. He
turns to Woody.*

MAX

How much time we got, Wood?

WOODY
(*checks his watch*)

Two minutes.

MAX

Bring me some more ketchup.
(*points to the Band-Aid on his head*)
And make this look real.

EXT. AUDITORIUM – NIGHT

*The lobby of the auditorium is buzzing with people talking about the
play and having drinks.*

Mr Blume is standing alone outside, smoking a cigarette. It is snowing softly. Miss Cross comes out with a cup of coffee in each hand. Mr Blume turns around and looks at her.

She goes over to him and hands him one of the coffees.

> MR BLUME
> (*sadly*)

Thank you.

> MISS CROSS

Hold this one, too, Herman.

He holds both coffees while Miss Cross pours some little containers of cream into them and stirs them with a plastic straw. She takes back her cup of coffee.

So what do you think of Max's latest opus?

Mr Blume gives a thumbs up and stares out into the snow.

> MR BLUME

Let's just hope it's got a happy ending.

Miss Cross smiles. She smooths her hand across Mr Blume's hair. He looks into her eyes. She links arms with him gently, and they drink their coffees together.

INT. AUDITORIUM – NIGHT

Max and Magnus Buchan, with a three-day beard and a cigar, stand together among the fallen bodies and smoldering trees.

> MAX

I want you to have something, Sarge.

Max hands Magnus Mr Blume's silver .45 automatic.

I won't be needing it anymore.

> MAGNUS

Semper fi, Esposito. Semper fi.

> MAX

Sic transit gloria, sir.

Max looks out to Mr Blume. Mr Blume looks back at him.

Say a prayer for Surf Boy. Wherever he is.

MAGNUS

Good luck, soldier.

Magnus salutes Max and walks off. We hear his voice as he goes into the wings:

Tag 'em and bag 'em, cherries! We're moving out! Let's DD!

Max throws down his rifle into a foxhole and begins to cry quietly. Someone moves slowly toward him out of the settling smoke. Max wheels around and whips out his Swiss Army knife.

But then he sees it is Margaret Yang as a Vietnamese villager. She has been through hell.

MARGARET

Hello, Esposito.

Max drops his knife and it stabs into the floor. He puts out his hand. Margaret takes it. He pulls her in and hugs her.

Miss Cross smiles sadly.

Max looks into Margaret Yang's eyes.

MAX

Will you marry me, Le-Chahn?

MARGARET
(*instantly*)

You bet I will.

Wagner's Flight of the Valkyries *begins to play loudly from behind the stage as Max kisses Margaret and the curtain drops to wild applause.*

Mrs Guggenheim looks on in amazement as Dr Guggenheim stands up out of his wheelchair and leads the ovation. The rest of the audience quickly follows suit.

The Indian Groundskeeper is laughing hysterically.

INT. GYMNASIUM – NIGHT

The gymnasium has been filled with palm trees and decorated like an army barracks. Flares burn in circles around the tables. A banner at the entrance says 'The Heaven and Hell Cotillion'.

Dirk and a couple of his Classmates are looking at some vintage Playboy *centerfolds taped up on the wall as part of the army barracks motif.*

Miss Cross and John are talking at the punchbowl.

> MISS CROSS
>
> Max sent you an invitation?

> JOHN
>
> Yeah. And he told me to wear a tie.

Max and Margaret are drinking ginger ales and chatting with Mr Fischer and Mr and Mrs Yang.

> MAX
>
> Thank you, Mrs Yang. I actually wrote a different version of the story two years ago. But I couldn't get it done over at Rushmore.

> MRS YANG
>
> Why? Too political?

> MAX
>
> No. A kid got his finger blown off during rehearsals.

Max sees Mr Blume and Miss Cross approaching.

> Miss Cross, this is my father, Bert Fischer. He's a barber.
> (*to Mr Fischer*)
> This is my friend Rosemary Cross.

Mr Fischer smiles as they shake hands.

> MR FISCHER
>
> Hi, Rosemary.

> MISS CROSS
>
> Nice to finally meet you, Bert.

MAX

And, of course, you know Mr Blume. I also want everyone to
meet Mr and Mrs Yang. And this is Margaret.

Miss Cross and Margaret smile at each other.

MISS CROSS

Hello, Margaret.

MARGARET

Nice to meet you, Miss Cross.

*The Indian Groundskeeper is talking with Coach Beck and Mr Blume's
foreman, Ernie.*

COACH BECK

I'm surprised they let him build a real campfire onstage.
That's a safety hazard.

ERNIE

Well, last year he tried to raise piranhas.

COACH BECK

What'd you think, Mr Littlejeans?

GROUNDSKEEPER

Best play all year, man.

*Mr Blume, Magnus Buchan and Max's young architect are having a
conversation.*

MAGNUS

Well, Fischer stepped on half my bleedin' lines.

MR BLUME

Really? I didn't notice.

ARCHITECT

Are Ronny and Donny having a good time at military school?

MR BLUME
(*instantly*)

They love it.

MAGNUS

Lucky bastards.

Mr Fischer is talking with John.

> JOHN
> I understand you're a neurosurgeon.

> MR FISCHER
> No. I'm a barber. But a lot of people make that mistake.

Mr Fischer laughs.

*Dirk and Dr Guggenheim watch Max laughing and dancing with
Margaret Yang. Max points to Dr Guggenheim. Dr Guggenheim smiles
and points back to him. He says in a hoarse whisper:*

> MR GUGGENHEIM
> Who's the Chinaman with Fischer?

> DIRK
> That's Margaret Yang. She's actually Korean.

> DR GUGGENHEIM
> (*pleasantly surprised*)
> I know the Koreans. They're good people.

Max and Margaret are talking as they dance:

> MAX
> You were incredible tonight, Margaret. You *were* that poor
> girl.

> MARGARET
> Thank you. I loved it when you grabbed on to the bottom of
> the chopper as it was taking off.

> MAX
> That was totally improvized.

Margaret nods. They look at each other smiling.

> Can I ask you a question?

> MARGARET
> Of course.

> MAX
> Can you do an Australian accent?

Margaret looks puzzled. Max smiles.

I'm working on something that's set in the outback.

Mr Fischer is sitting at a table having a glass of champagne with Max's math teacher, Mrs Whitney. She has a slight English accent. Mr Fischer wears a sky-blue blazer.

MR FISCHER

That's a beautiful dress, by the way.

MRS WHITNEY

Why, thank you, Bert. That sports coat is rather smashing in its own right.

MR FISCHER

I know it's a little loud. But I feel like celebrating.

MRS WHITNEY

Would you care to dance?

MR FISCHER
(*surprised*)

I'd love to.

Mr Blume brings Miss Cross a glass of champagne as Max and Margaret dance by.

MARGARET

Hello, Mr Blume!

MR BLUME

Hi, Margaret!
(*to Max*)

May I cut in? I haven't had a chance to cut a rug with your new girlfriend yet.

MAX
(*embarrassed*)

New girlfriend.

MARGARET

Yes, I am. And find your own dance partner, Mr Blume. No offense, but I'm spoken for.

                              MAX
        No, it's OK. He's my friend.

*Margaret and Mr Blume dance off together. Max and Miss Cross are
left alone.*

                         MISS CROSS
        Well, you pulled it off.

                              MAX
                           (*shrugs*)
        It went OK. At least nobody got hurt.

                         MISS CROSS
        Except for you.

                              MAX
                        (*smiles sadly*)
        Nah. I didn't get hurt that bad.

*Max looks to Miss Cross. Miss Cross sips her champagne. She looks
back at Max for a minute. She smiles. Mr Fischer calls out to them as
he dances by with Mrs Whitney:*

                         MR FISCHER
        Come on, you two! Shake a leg!

They wave to Mr Fischer. Miss Cross looks to Max.

                         MISS CROSS
        You want to dance?

                              MAX
        Certainly. But let's see if we can get the DJ to play something
        with a little –

Max snaps his fingers. He turns to the DJ and yells:

        Reuben!

*The DJ looks to Max. Max makes a little gesture that seems to say,
This is the one. The DJ nods.*

*The music cuts off in the middle of the song. Everyone stops dancing.
They look around wondering what's going on.*

A new song starts up. It is the saddest song of the night.

Max looks to Miss Cross. Miss Cross puts out her hand. Max takes it and walks with her on to the dance floor, into the crowd, as everyone slowly begins to dance.

Credits

Concierge	MICHAEL MAGGART
Isaac	ROBBIE LEE
Bellman	MORGAN REDMOND
Security Guard	ED GELDART
Dynamite Salesman	DAVID MORITZ
Tommy Stalling	J. J. KILLALEA
Mr Yang	WILLIAM LAU
Mrs Yang	LUCILLE SADIKIN
Tennis Pro	STEVE ECKELMAN
Architect	ERIC ANDERSON
Coach Fritz	DANNY FINE
Regis	KYLE RYAN URQUHART
Mr LittleJeans	KUMAR PALLANA
Reuben	STEPHEN DIGNAN
Stunt Coordinator	DAVID SANDERS

THE FILM-MAKERS

Directed by	WES ANDERSON
Written by	WES ANDERSON and OWEN WILSON
Produced by	BARRY MENDEL and PAUL SCHIFF
Director of Photography	ROBERT YEOMAN
Production Designer	DAVID WASCO
Editor	DAVID MORITZ
Costume Designer	KAREN PATCH
Executive Producers	WES ANDERSON and OWEN WILSON
Co-Producer	JOHN CAMERON
Music by	MARK MOTHERSBAUGH
Casting by	MARY GAIL ARTZ and BARBARA COHEN
Music Supervisor	RANDALL POSTER
Unit Production Manager	JOHN CAMERON
First Assistant Director	MICHAEL CEDAR
Second Assistant Director	CONTE MATAL
Set Decorator	ALEXANDRA REYNOLDS-WASCO
Script Supervisor	SCOTT PETERSON
Sound Mixer	PAWEL WDOWCZAK
Art Director	ANDREW LAWS
Assistant Art Director	AUSTIN GORG
Assistant Set Decorator	AMANDA ANDERSON
On-Set Dresser	EVELYN COLLEEN SARO
Greens Coordinator	WALLACE R. SYMS

Leadman	JEFFREY B. HARTMAN
Costume Supervisor	CATHERINE ALLEN BUSCH
On-Set Costumer	JENNIFER LONG
Costumer	LEEANN RADEKA
Wardrobe Assistant	JAMELLE FLOWERS
Animation & Models Furnished by	HALO PRODUCTIONS
Animator	DAVID RIDLEN
Key Hair/Make-Up	ROBERT W. HARPER
	SALLY J. HARPER
Hair/Make-Up Stylist	THERESA HARPER
Mr Murray's Hair/Make-Up	FRANCES HANNON
Prosthetic Make-Up Artist	BART J. MIXON
First Assistant Camera	JOHN BOCCACCIO
Second Assistant Camera	JIMMY W. LINDSEY
Loader	VAL SKLAR
Boom Operator	DAVID SMITH
Cable/Utility	SCOTT STREETMAN
First Assistant Editor	DANIEL R. PADGETT
Assistant Editors	TERRY HUBBARD
	LIN COLEPERSON
Apprentice Editor	RON RADVINSKY
Music Editor	MICHAEL BABER
Supervising Sound Editor	JOHN NUTT
Sound Effects Designer	KYRSTEN MATE COMOGLIO
Sound Effects Editor	AURA GILGE
Assistant Sound Effects Editor	YIN CANTOR
Dialogue Editor	DAVID FRANKLIN BERGAD
Foley Editor	MALCOLM FIFE
Additional Voices Performed by	LOOP TROOPR
ADR Recordist	DOC KANE
Loop Group Editor	LARRY MANN
Foley Artists	MARGIE O'MALLEY
	MARNIE MOOR
Foley Mixer	STEVEN FONTANO
Foley Recordist	FRANK RINELLA
Supervising Rerecording Mixer	MARK BERGER
Rerecording Mixer	MICHAEL SEMANICK
Rerecording Room Supervisor	GRANT FOERSTER
Machine Room Operator	JIM PASQUE
Sound Editing, Foley &	
Rerecording at	THE SAUL ZAENTZ FILM CENTER
Rigging Gaffer	PETER CLARSON

132

Rigging Best Boy Electric	CHERYL CLARSON
Electricians	EDISON JACKSON
	W. K. MACTAVISH II
	DANNY NAVARETTE
	KEVIN SIMS
Best Boy Electric	BUZZY BURWELL
Key Grip	FERRELL A. SHINNICK
Best Boy Grip	MICHAEL SHEEREN
Dolly Grip	DOUG CHARTIER
Key Rigging Grip	DENNIS CLAY
Best Boy Rigging Grip	DOUG MERCER
Grips	LAYNE CHANEY
	STEVEN GUERRERO
	SEAN R. WRIGHT
Rigging Grip	KURT KORNEMANN
Gaffer	VOYA MIKULIC
Propmaster	MELISSA MATTHIES
Assistant Propmasters	DAVID M. BOWEN
	RIK TRZECIAK
Special Effects Coordinator	RON TROST
Production Supervisor	CHRISTINE FRANSEN
Production Coordinator	MELISSA WIECHMANN
Assistant Production Coordinator	STEPHEN LIGHT
Second Second Assistant Director	DONALD W. MURPHY
Assistant to Mr Anderson	MOIRA C. GILL
Assistant to Mr Mendel (Texas)	MONICA ANN ALLEN
Assistant to Mr Mendel (LA)	JENNIFER SIMPSON
Assistant to Mr Schiff (Texas)	TED BRODEN
Assistant to Mr Schiff (LA)	JASON HAWKINS
Assistant to Mr Schwartzman	STEVE ECKELMAN
Set Designer	DANIEL BRADFORD
Construction Coordinator	ROY METCALF
Construction Foreman	CHAD LOUCKS
Locations Manager	CRAIG ALLEN BUSCH
Assistant Locations Manager	VIRGINIA DIAZ
Art Department Assistants	DAVID MELITO
	NICOLE GORG
Production Assistants	CARRIE ALBERS
	JONATHAN HENNESSEY
	LINELL KATHLEEN TOWNES
	VICTOR LACOUR
	JESSICA DAILEY

133

Teacher	CECILIA M. CARDWELL
Stand-In for Miss Williams	ANGELA LAUX
Accountant	MICHAEL GRIGSBY
First Assistant Accountant	RIP RUSSELL
Payroll Accountant	LINDA BRATTAIN
Post Production Accountant	LYDIA CEDRONE
Publicist	TAMMY LORKOVIC
Still Photographer	VAN REDIN
24 Frame Playback	PETER VERRANDO
Transportation Coordinator	RON KERN
Transportation Captain	MARTIN WELLS
Transportation Co-Captain	FRED DAVIS
Casting Associate	DEBRA SECHER
Local Casting	LIZ KEIGLEY
Extras Casting	BETH SEPKO
Animal Wrangler	DOUG TERRANOVA
Bee Wranglers	KALEN HOYLE
	MICHAEL R. WOHLFELD
Dog Trainer	RENEE ROTH
Medic	VICKI DANIELS JOHNSON
Calligrapher	MARK VAN STONE
Executive in charge of Music for the Buena Vista Motion Pictures Group	KATHY NELSON
Score Recorded by	ROBERT CASALE
Score Recorded at	MUTATO MUZIKA, WEST HOLLYWOOD, CA
Orchestrations by	MARK MOTHERSBAUGH
Musician Contractor	DANPING WONG
Music Coordinator	CHRIS PARKER
Titles and Opticals by	PACIFIC TITLE
Negative Cutting	BUENA VISTA NEGATIVE CUTTING
Color Timer	GLORIA KAISER
Additional Casting	JUEL BESTROP
	DEBRA ZANE

SONGS

'MAKING TIME'
Written by Edwin Michael Phillips & Kenneth George Pickett
Published by EMI UNART Catalog Inc. (BMI)
Performed by Creation
Courtesy of Shel Talmy Entertainment